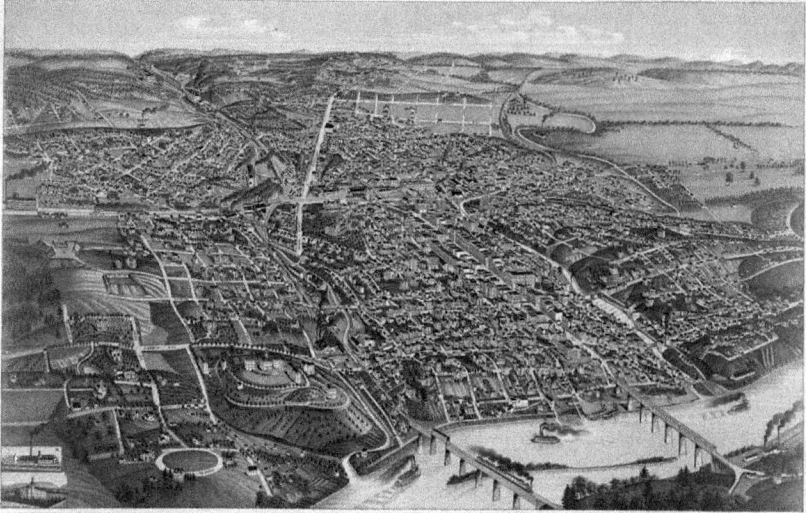

KNOXVILLE, TENN.

COUNTY SEAT OF KNOX COUNTY.

1886.

Population, 60,000.

A bird's-eye view of the booming city of Knoxville in 1886. During that decade, the mostly industrial city more than doubled in size. *Courtesy of the Library of Congress.*

# KNOXVILLE

## THIS OBSCURE PRISMATIC CITY

### JACK NEELY

THE
History
PRESS

Published by The History Press
Charleston, SC 29403
www.historypress.net

First published 2009
Second printing 2013

*Cover image*: "Gay Street Bridge" by Mike C. Berry. www.mikecberry.com.

ISBN 9781540219787

Library of Congress Cataloging-in-Publication Data

Neely, Jack.
Knoxville : this obscure prismatic city / Jack Neely.
p. cm.
ISBN 9781540219787
1. Knoxville (Tenn.)--Biography--Anecdotes. 2. Knoxville (Tenn.)--History--
Miscellanea. I. Title.
F444.K7N438 2009
976.8'85--dc22
2009041866

# CONTENTS

# THE BLOUNT CONSPIRACY

K noxville would not exist as a city if not for a man from North Carolina named William Blount. James White and his family and allies were the first to settle here, and White played an important role in organizing the early settlers on this bluff above what was then known as the Holston. But it was Blount, signer of the U.S. Constitution and governor of the new Southwestern Territory, who decided that one of dozens of pioneer settlements along the watersheds west of the Alleghenies should be his territorial capital and, therefore, something like a city.

It was Blount who named Knoxville "Knoxville," after his friend and, significantly, superior, Henry Knox, President Washington's secretary of war and de facto supervisor of the new republic's territories. And it was Blount who orchestrated the boldest plot against his country's interests in the history of the U.S. Senate.

In 1796, the former Southwestern Territory achieved statehood as Tennessee, with some help from Blount, who became one of the new state's first senators.

By then, Blount, resident of Blount Mansion, Hill Avenue, Knoxville, had seen half a decade as governor of a nearly ungovernable territory, dealing with angry Indians, French secret agents, drunken backwoodsmen and frontier democrats. After that experience, the U.S. Senate must have seemed dull, even compared to the Constitutional Convention in Philadelphia, through which Blount had dozed a decade earlier.

Land was what moved William Blount, and he owned lots of it across Tennessee to the Mississippi River. Western Tennessee's potential depended on the river remaining free for commerce all the way to the Gulf. Spain controlled Louisiana and the river, but the European kingdom had lost a war

William Blount, signer of the U.S. Constitution and governor of the Southwestern Territory, established his capital in Knoxville, effectively making the tiny frontier settlement an important political center. In midlife, his career took a couple of bizarre turns. *Courtesy of the Library of Congress.*

to France, where Napoleon was rising rapidly to power. It seemed clear that France—revolutionary, pre-dictatorial France—was soon to seize Louisiana and choke the Mississippi's precious barge traffic.

The answer to this real-estate dilemma might have seemed clear to any red-blooded Knoxvillian. Get the Creek, Choctaw and Cherokee Indians and a few disgruntled Tories and reckless frontier adventurers on your side. Then make a secret alliance with Great Britain, your new nation's recent enemy but the greatest naval power in the world. Then, blitz the Spanish! Conquer Louisiana for King George III! How could you lose?

As it turned out, Tennessee whiskey had something to do with it.

Only a few of Blount's closest associates knew the whole plot. One was John Chisholm, the rough-edged Scottish-born adventurer, by some accounts a former British soldier, whose capacious and accommodating tavern stood near Blount Mansion.

Another was Dr. Nicholas Romayne, medical professor at New York's University of Columbia, described by historians as "a strange, interesting man, erudite but emotional, calculating but rash, enormous but indefatigable, a 300-pound phenomenon with a light, precise step." Though Romayne lived in New York, he seems to have had a keen interest in the Tennessee frontier and Blount's schemes.

# This Obscure Prismatic City

In 1795, the professor and the governor had hatched a secret real-estate plan to "lay out a large city, two miles square," in the vicinity of the relatively small settlement of Knoxville. The frontier metropolis, touted as a haven for European immigrants, would be called "Palmyra."

They kept it in "profound Secrecy," by Blount's phrasing, pending the purchase of more than one thousand acres necessary to get it started. Known only through a few letters, the details of its apparent collapse are obscure. By 1797, Blount, Romayne and Chisholm had outlined a much more audacious plan.

By some accounts Romayne took the scheme to London, while Chisholm attempted to make headway with a fellow Brit, foreign minister John Liston. "Let me be plain, Jack," he wrote. "I will conquer or be damned." Chisholm told some British officials that Blount would personally lead an army of frontiersmen to invade New Orleans. Chisholm would lead an army of Indians against Spanish positions in Pensacola. Britain would gain Florida and the broad Louisiana territory and guarantee that the Mississippi would remain open to river commerce.

Several versions of the story unfolded over a period of months. They may all be true. By some accounts, Chisholm and other leaders of the plan were commissioned as British officers. Senator Blount, in particular, wanted to be the British governor of Louisiana.

The skeptical Lord Grenville, already concerned that rumors of the plot had made their way to the Spanish ambassador, replied to Blount and company, sorry, he rather thought not.

Meanwhile, Blount's ill-chosen secret agent among the Indians, James Carey, got drunk and blabbed. He showed off an incriminating letter he had received from Senator Blount. David Henley, agent of the War Department in Knoxville, caught wind of the plot and sent the letter directly to recently inaugurated President Adams, who demanded an investigation.

The story goes that on July 3, 1797, Senator Blount walked into the Senate chamber innocently, just as the clerk was reading Blount's own incriminating letter. Vice President Thomas Jefferson ambushed Blount with questions about the message. Blount replied that he wasn't sure whether he had written it or not. He slipped out of the capital—by one account, he stowed away on a southbound freighter—and made his way overland to the rough safety of Tennessee.

The U.S. Senate expelled Blount from its ranks by an overwhelming vote and then sent the sergeant-at-arms down here to fetch the traitor to face criminal charges. Blount refused to leave Tennessee, and the government man couldn't get up a posse in Blount's Knoxville to force him back. Blount entertained the man with a dinner in Blount Mansion before his guest returned to the capital empty-handed.

Blount Mansion, built in 1792, was home to William Blount and his wife, Mary. It was the first frame house west of the Appalachian Mountains and perhaps the first with glass windows. This photo shows the site as it appeared in the mid-twentieth century, after preservationists saved it from being razed for parking in 1925. *Courtesy of the Library of Congress.*

Former president George Washington denounced Blount's "nefarious conduct," suggesting that Blount "be held in detestation by all good men." Tennesseans ignored that advice, electing Blount to the state legislature, which then met in Knoxville, the new state's capital.

Chisholm eventually left town; his further adventures on the frontier are little known. Dr. Romayne was arrested in New York and imprisoned for a time. Upon his release in 1798, he exiled himself to Edinburgh, where he became the first American professor at the Royal College of Physicians. He later returned to America and founded the College of Physicians and Surgeons in New York.

Blount was content to remain Knoxville's most popular fugitive from justice. Accounts weren't settled until March 1800, when, suffering one of the fevers of the day, he collapsed on his piazza at Blount Mansion. He died only a couple of weeks after word reached Knoxville that Napoleon had seized control of France.

After more than two centuries, much of the Blount Conspiracy remains a thick, dark mystery. The only evidence we have today are a few fragmentary letters and, overlooking the river, a nice old, white, clapboard house, the one the Cherokees once called "the House with Many Eyes." It ain't talking.

# THE CURIOUS PROFESSOR

It was just the sixth day of June 1868 and already it was the most uncomfortable summer in memory. Knoxvillians were fleeing their hometown by the dozens. At the depot at the foot of Immaculate Conception's hill, the trains heading north were more crowded than they'd ever been.

The flags at the courthouse and post office were at half-mast after the first news that President Buchanan was dead. To add to the executive-level distress, Democratic president Andrew Johnson was being impeached by Congress.

Whether that was good news in Knoxville was a complicated question. The Knoxville district's popular representative in Congress, Horace Maynard, was generally an ally of his pro-impeachment Republicans.

To relieve the heat and the stress of living in Knoxville in the summer of 1868, downtown hotel saloons were offering their usual ales and porters, plus a new concoction: the Impeachment Cocktail. Recipes are elusive.

William G. "Parson" Brownlow, the exuberantly tactless editor of the *Knoxville Whig* who, surprisingly, was also the governor of Tennessee, had been ill. The word on Gay Street was that Parson—the formerly anti-black, anti-Catholic, anti-Confederate, anti-Presbyterian Parson—was finally dead.

In Chattanooga, Father Abram Ryan, the young, wild-haired "Poet-Priest of the Confederacy" who had known Brownlow when he lived in Knoxville as the priest at Immaculate Conception, came up with a fun little rhyme celebrating Parson's descent into hell. Knoxvillians gleefully recited Ryan's verse.

But Parson was hardly dead at all, even if he had always sort of looked it. In response to Father Ryan's premature eulogy, Brownlow's *Whig* condemned the cleric as a "drunken, corrupt, Catholic priest."

The biggest event that Saturday was the horse race just after midday dinner. Bus-sized carriages ferried Knoxvillians from downtown hotels to the racetrack a couple of miles out of town to the west. In the first race, Sparrow Hawk beat Cricket by a length and a half. But then the sky turned dark and the wind picked up, blowing up thick billows of dust. The rest of the day's races were postponed. Even downtown, the strange wind stirred dust so thick that men sipping Impeachment Cocktails at the St. Nicholas could only see half a block up Gay or down Cumberland. A hard rain followed, effectively coating everything in Knoxville in a thin layer of mud.

On Immaculate Conception Hill, men working with shovels could see the horse-drawn trolleys bringing racing enthusiasts back to town via Asylum Avenue. As the sudden storm subsided, these workers resumed their grading work on Vine Avenue, the street that went up the hill to the church, shoveling the wet dirt to take out some of the steepness of the grade on the eastern slope. At about 4:00 p.m., one workman lifted a shovel, and there, in the clay, lay part of a human being.

Soon, the workers unearthed the rest of the skeleton, that of an adult man who had been resting there for some forty years. The sight of dirty human remains probably didn't shock anybody who saw it. In 1868, Knoxvillians were all too accustomed to the sight of corpses, especially those of men who had died violently. Still, at the hotel saloons there was no shortage of speculation about whom these bones belonged to and how they came to arrive on that spot on the hillside. Some had heard something about a graveyard for slaves there, long since abandoned.

At length, an elderly man who had surveyed the bones on the hill stepped forward with some authority to tell a story that was much stranger than any of the rumors.

The old man was recognized as a long-retired Knoxville sheriff who remembered the days before there was a Catholic church on the hill, when it was outside of Knoxville's city limits. He remembered when there was a gallows up there. And he remembered the eccentric professor at the university who once tried to restore life to the body of an executed murderer.

Much of the story of Knoxville's Dr. Frankenstein is lost to us now, many of its details decayed with the years, almost like flesh. What we know comes through the memories of George White, as recorded that hot June, forty years afterward. That day he told only the end of the yarn. He may not have known the beginning of it, which took place across the ocean, in another century.

# This Obscure Prismatic City

By the late 1700s, about the time Knoxville was founded, an Italian physicist named Luigi Galvani was startling the scientific community with his experiments with electricity. With makeshift electric batteries, Galvani proved that he could use electrical currents to cause reactions in animal tissue. He could, for example, make frog legs jump. An English scientist, Erasmus Darwin, grandfather of Charles, was equally intrigued with the idea of such reanimation, if less successfully than Galvani, though Darwin claimed to have induced "voluntary motion" in a piece of vermicelli.

Galvani died in 1798, but his nephew, Luigi Aldini, carried on his legacy. By 1803, Aldini had shown that he could liven up parts of an ox's severed head by applying electrodes in carefully selected spots.

Next in the scientific lineage of test subjects, of course, would be humans. Aldini obtained permission to send a few jolts through a freshly hanged murderer. He had some success, causing the corpse to open one eye and clench a fist. Over the next several years, the European dead were in great demand as subjects, as excited scientists in several countries shocked corpses, provoking them to twitch, jump, sit up, even breathe. So far, though, their goal of restoring actual life to a dead body eluded them.

Especially fascinated with those experiments was the nineteen-year-old daughter of a well-known feminist author; the teenager had recently married the poet Percy Shelley. In 1816, Mary Wollstonecraft Shelley and her husband were in Switzerland vacationing with Lord Byron and a young physician named John Polidori and found themselves discussing the state-of-the-art corpse-shocking fad. Stuck inside during the cold, wet summer, the four had a little contest to see who could write the spookiest story. Dr. Polidori told a story of the evil dead. He later published it as a novel, called *The Vampyre*.

Mary came up with a yarn about an obsessed scientist who finally succeeds in reanimating corpseflesh. Her novel, *Frankenstein*, emerged in 1818 and soon became a worldwide sensation. In her preface to the novel, Mary Shelley assures readers that what she describes is scientifically plausible.

*Frankenstein* was well known in Tennessee by the summer of 1828, when young Sheriff White prepared a gallows on the hill. It was then the northern city limits of the forlorn former state capital and unlikely to offend. There, White proposed to hang two murderers. One was an old man who had killed his wife with an axe. The other was a man in his thirties who had killed his lover's husband. A crowd gathered, many of whom were women grieving that such a young, handsome lover should be removed from their midst so suddenly.

At East Tennessee College, which was just that summer moving from its original Gay Street campus to its hallowed hill on the west side of town, was an unusual young professor named Stephen Foster. Known to his students as "the Learned Foster," he was a man of liberal curiosities. A Presbyterian minister, the thirty-year-old scholar had assembled one of the town's first "Galvanic" batteries, inspired by Luigi Galvani. Apparently a pretty sizeable object, it was installed at the Second Presbyterian Church, then located on Prince Street, which would many years later be known as Market.

On the day of the hanging, Professor Foster made an unusual deal with Sheriff White. Up on the hill, barely within sight of the simple chapel of Second Presbyterian, two murderers stood on a horse-drawn cart with nooses around their necks. It was Sheriff White who shouted, "Giddyap!"

When he was satisfied that the dangling men were sincerely dead, White cut down the bodies. One, the old man, was buried on site but perhaps not very deep. It was he, White thought forty years later, who had been subject to the graders' unceremonious exhumation.

The other unfortunate, the young man, the heartthrob "in the very vigor of manhood," the sheriff recalled, was hastily loaded onto a one-horse cart—perhaps the same one the condemned man had been standing on moments earlier—and sped down the hill to Second Presbyterian. They hauled his limp body into the church itself, where Professor Foster and his impressive battery waited. The doors closed on the expectant crowd.

One man scaled the outside wall of the church and peered through a transom. He reported the proceedings within to the anxious throng.

Professor Foster laid out the still-warm corpse of the handsome young murderer. Carefully, Foster applied electrodes to the cooling flesh and completed the circuit.

A rare image of the Second Presbyterian Church at Clinch Avenue and Market Street, as it appeared in the 1820s, when it doubled as a library for Professor Stephen Foster's experiments in galvanism. *Detail from a postcard in the collection of Mark Heinz.*

# This Obscure Prismatic City

The gravestone of Presbyterian minister—and university physics professor—Stephen Foster (1798–1835), known in the 1820s for his experiments with using electricity to reanimate tissue of the recently deceased. The inscription ends, "Mysterious are thy ways, O Lord." *Photo by the author.*

The dead man moved. The corpse breathed once, twice, three times. The spy at the transom reported Professor Foster's success to the crowd below, and a cheer went up in the dusty streets of Knoxville. Professor Foster, it appeared, had found a solution to death.

But then Professor Foster put his electrodes away and turned his experiment over to the dead man's family. This Presbyterian minister had no intention to cheat the law, he said, and bring a condemned killer back to life. He merely wished to satisfy his "philosophical curiosity…as to the effects of galvanism on the human body."

Professor Foster himself died young, still in his thirties. He's buried at the churchyard on State Street beneath a stone inscribed, "Mysterious are thy ways, O Lord." As for his subject, his family reportedly buried him at their home in another county. Of course, no one knows for certain.

Forty years later, Knoxvillians listening to Sheriff White's strange yarn were much more sophisticated about how much activity could be expected from a dead body. But the next time they saw the formerly deceased Parson Brownlow loping down Cumberland Avenue and looking even more cadaverous than he used to, they must have taken hard swigs of their Impeachment Cocktails and wondered.

# THESE HONORED DEAD

At about three o'clock on a Thursday afternoon, the president of the formerly United States stepped up to a podium to dedicate a freshly dug cemetery in Pennsylvania. Numbering in the tens of thousands, the crowd on hand was perhaps the largest crowd ever to witness the dedication of a cemetery. It was not as big as the crowd that had been buried under the earth at Gettysburg in the four months since the battle.

As Abraham Lincoln rose to speak on the afternoon of November 19, 1863, he didn't yet know about one casualty, one whose promotion to brigadier general he had approved only four weeks before. About four hundred miles to the southwest, as the crow flies, many of Gettysburg's Confederate veterans, those not yet buried, were hurling themselves against another forbidding Federal defense. Just the afternoon before, a very young Union general facing that assault had fallen to the ground with a Confederate Minié ball in his gut.

As Lincoln stood at the podium and spoke with reverence of "these honored dead," William Pitt Sanders, barely thirty years old, lay dead in a big double bed in the bridal suite of the Lamar House, the most posh hotel on Gay Street.

Sanders's men carried him there after he was wounded, using a ladder for a stretcher. He was conscious, and it was there at the Lamar House where he learned he would soon die. Like an ancient Greek warrior, Sanders thanked God that he bore his wound in the front. That morning, the Kentucky-born, Mississippi-raised Sanders earned an awful distinction: of all the generals who died fighting for the Union, Sanders was the only born-and-raised Southerner.

Brigadier General William Sanders (1833–1963). Only thirty and recently promoted, Sanders was mortally wounded by the advancing Confederates on Kingston Pike, just west of the city. He was the only Southern-born Union general to die in the war. *Courtesy of the National Archives.*

The Lamar House, as it appeared during an occasion of some interest (historians argue about which one), probably soon after the Civil War. Built in 1816, the Lamar House was Knoxville's finest hostelry of the Civil War era and included a popular saloon on the ground floor. It was where mortally wounded General William Sanders was brought to die and where the young officer's body lay as his commanding general suppressed the news of his death. The building now serves as the front portion of the Bijou Theatre. *Calvin McClung Historical Collection.*

# This Obscure Prismatic City

When Lincoln spoke at Gettysburg, Sanders had been dead for five hours. By then, the Confederates held the hill that he had defended with his life.

That afternoon on frantic Gay Street, soldiers and citizens, both black and white, hastened to shore up the Union defenses against the siege. Knoxville was surrounded by fifteen thousand Confederate troops, most of them entrenched within a mile of the city. From the top of the Lamar House, it would have been easy to see their lines, their tents and the glint of their bayonets in every direction over land.

Almost no one in the streets knew the truth about the tall, bearded general they had seen on his white charger only yesterday. For days, Sanders's death would be a secret—from the enemy, from the townspeople and from his own men. In two months of Federal occupation, Sanders had become such an icon of Union bravery that General Burnside feared the news of his death would be a crippling blow to morale at the worst time. He ordered that no one divulge the fact of Sanders's death. Sanders would be buried in silence long after nightfall in an unmarked grave in a churchyard on Prince Street, much later to be known as Market Street.

At an appointed hour near midnight, a small cadre of officers bore their comrade's body out of the Lamar House by lantern light, barely four blocks away to the churchyard of Second Presbyterian, the tall-steepled church near Market Square. Orlando Poe, the genius of Knoxville's formidable earthen defenses, had been a close friend of Sanders since their days at West Point. At the graveyard, Poe defied Burnside's order of silence and raised his pistol in the air to lead a volley of sidearm fire that echoed through Market Square and surely startled nervous sleepers in this city under siege.

Officially, the word on the street in Knoxville—and the word reported on the front pages of New York newspapers—was that Sanders was still recovering from a bad wound.

Up until then, the Federal earthworks at the summit of a ridge half a mile west of Prince Street had been known as Fort Loudoun. It must have seemed an odd name for the largest Federal fort in the region; Fort Loudoun had been an ill-fated British fort in the French and Indian War, by then a rarely seen ruin about thirty miles away on the Little Tennessee. The Union army's tradition, observed in all of the other, smaller forts that ringed Knoxville, was to name them after Union officers who had died in the East Tennessee campaigns. At Poe's suggestion, Fort Loudoun was rechristened Fort Sanders—just in time for the November 29 battle that earned national headlines and ended Longstreet's adventures in East Tennessee.

(Today there is no graveyard on Market Street. About forty years after Sanders's burial it was moved, its graves relocated to other cemeteries, mostly in town. The whereabouts of General Sanders's grave puzzled a generation or

A somewhat fanciful painting of the Battle of Fort Sanders—a disastrous twenty-minute Confederate charge in November 1863 that ended a month-long siege conducted by General James Longstreet. *Courtesy of the Library of Congress.*

two of twentieth-century historians until someone noticed his name on a simple government-issue headstone at the main military cemetery in Chattanooga. No one knows how he ended up there.)

The Friday, November 20 edition of the *New York Times* reported the top news of the day: "IMPORTANT NEWS FROM EAST TENNESSEE—The Rebel Army Advancing Upon Knoxville." The lead paragraph read, "The enemy began skirmishing from their position on the Kingston Road…A desperate charge was made…Gen. SANDERS was severely wounded, and was borne from the field."

Sharing the front page with less emphasis was the day's second-biggest story: "THE HEROES OF JULY—A Solemn and Imposing Event—Dedication of the National Cemetery at Gettysburg." Included were some details of a short speech given by the president.

# THE QUIET PASSENGER

A mumbled word, an unexplained death, a missing manuscript: this may be the strangest story in the history of American literature. Though the competition is tougher, it's one of the strangest stories in the history of Gay Street.

It came to pass in the last month of Tennessee's most violent decade. George Washington Harris was fifty-five, one of America's most popular humorists and at the top of his game in 1869. For fifteen years, the adventures of his reckless character, Sut Lovingood, had been read aloud, told and retold from New York to San Francisco, drawing horselaughs from urban and rural audiences alike. Sut was Huck Finn on amphetamines—a manic, perverse child of some backwoods holler where Idiocy and Genius merge into one.

For most of his life, Sut's creator had lived in Knoxville and had enjoyed a diversity of careers. He had been a riverboat pilot, a horse-racing jockey, a jeweler, an industrialist and the city postmaster. He had been involved in local Democratic Party politics for years. All the while, he wrote his stories. Most were set in the remote countryside of southeastern Tennessee, but a few were set in downtown Knoxville. In "A Razor-Grinder in a Thunderstorm," Sut describes no-nonsense Knoxville, circa 1850, as the best place "for sweepin out the inside of stuffed-up fellers' skulls clean of all ole rusty, cobweb, bigoted ideas…and then a-fillin it up fresh with something new and active"—including, in the story, a determination never to return to Knoxville.

Considering the heedless, uninhibited nature of most of Harris's stories, which treated law, sex, religion and death irreverently, it may seem surprising that conservative Knoxville newspapers were Harris's first and most dependable market.

It may also be surprising, considering that Harris's stories suggest little respect for organized religion, that Harris was an elder in the First Presbyterian Church.

He had left town around 1860, likely with some encouragement from his Unionist neighbors. Harris the secessionist had moved to the real South: Nashville and then Georgia. In 1869, Harris lived in Alabama, where his anti-Republican virulence was less likely to get him in trouble. But even in Alabama, Harris wrote mainly about East Tennessee and still published some of his stories first in the Knoxville newspaper. The Democratic one, of course.

Harris's 1867 collection, *Sut Lovingood's Yarns*, was a national success. For a California paper, a young journalist named Sam Clemens gave the book a favorable review. In the meantime, Harris kept up his newspaper work, which seemed only to get better. In the *Knoxville Press & Messenger* in 1868, he published what some scholars would later regard as his best story, "Bill Ainsworth's Quarter Race," apparently based on his own experiences as a teenage jockey at Mr. Nance's track in Knoxville.

Harris's strangest tale was published in the same paper a few weeks later. Calculated to give a funeral director terminal nightmares, it is a too-vivid description of a rowdy fiasco of a funeral service, a thoroughly uncivilized burial of a sort Harris may have concluded our species might deserve.

Clearly on a roll, Harris put together another collection, a sequel of sorts, and called it *High Times and Hard Times*. In late 1869, he packed it up and got on a train to Lynchburg, where he visited a prospective publisher. It's unclear how that meeting went, but Harris still had a copy of the manuscript with him when he got on the return train to Alabama. The trip would, coincidentally, take him through his old hometown.

As the train approached East Tennessee on that Saturday in December, the conductors worried about the snow on the tracks, maybe five inches deep. They also worried about the little man with the neat beard and the gold pocket watch sleeping in his seat. As they approached the Tennessee border, the man fell to the floor, unconscious. Assuming that he was drunk, the conductors laid him across two seats and, for the next several miles, argued about what to do with him. One conductor apparently ignored an order to dump him off at Bristol.

When an Atlanta businessman boarded at Bulls Gap, he recognized George Washington Harris, the famous author, and suggested that they find him help at the next major stop. At Morristown, the conductor tried to wake Harris again to ask him if he'd like to get off in Knoxville. This time, Harris roused enough to breathe the answer, "Yes," and then slipped back into senselessness.

New Market. Strawberry Plains. Then, Knoxville. The station was on the north end of Gay Street, at the bottom of the hill. At the time, it was just a

Influential author and humorist
George Washington Harris
(1814–1869), who may not have
known that his train had arrived
in his hometown at the time of his
mysterious death. *Courtesy of the
Library of Congress*.

small depot. Across the street was an unpretentious hotel called the Atkin House. Advertised as a railroad "Dinner House," with a restaurant and a whiskey bar, it was just the sort of place that Harris hated. He had lampooned rail-side roadhouses in a couple of stories, one called "Tripetown: Twenty Minutes for Breakfast."

Harris didn't care much at one o'clock that afternoon when hotel attendants carried him unconscious into a room in the Atkin. A little-known physician at the hotel, one Dr. Kraus, had a look at him and told a newspaper reporter that there wasn't much hope. His tentative diagnosis was "apoplexy," or stroke.

It would have been a peculiar night in Knoxville in any case. It was cold and windier than usual, and to the west, after the sun went down, was a strange orange glow, like a sunset that lasted far too long. It must be a huge fire, everyone downtown agreed, but no one had any clue what might be burning.

During the night, four other physicians arrived at the lantern-lit Atkin House to offer their own diagnoses of the unfortunate passenger. Among them was former Confederate surgeon John Mason Boyd, famous for his participation in one of the first successful hysterectomies in medical history. Another was dental surgeon John Fouché; as it happened, he was Harris's brother-in-law. The patient appeared to recognize Dr. Fouché and briefly regained consciousness, giving doctors hope that he might be rallying. Desperate for some clue about his condition, they persisted with diagnostic questions. In answer, George Harris was able to pronounce only one word that night. He said, "Poisoned."

That was about ten o'clock. Toward midnight, Harris died.

There was no autopsy. Disagreeing with Dr. Kraus's diagnosis, the other doctors present suggested "morphia," a medically ambiguous term that may have suggested a morphine overdose. A brief inquest on Sunday was inconclusive. Officially, George Washington Harris died of an "unknown cause."

Also unknown were the whereabouts of one significant piece of Harris's luggage. The author's main literary project during the last year of his life, the book manuscript *High Times and Hard Times*, was missing. Overlooked and forgotten in the sudden disorder of Harris's death, in the months and years to come, the unpublished book would frustrate several searches by family members and literary historians.

Posterity has been good to the memory of George Washington Harris. More than a century after his death, his stories are included in most major college-survey anthologies of American literature. He is generally regarded as America's funniest and most daring author before Twain. In one way or another, William Faulkner, Flannery O'Connor and Cormac McCarthy have acknowledged his influence.

Almost nothing remains of Harris's life and death in downtown Knoxville. The Atkin House and the old ETV&G station have been gone for more than a century. There is no trace of Nance's racetrack, nothing of the antebellum courthouse Harris made fun of in a couple of stories and no relic of the riverboats he piloted in the 1830s. None of the three or more houses Harris lived and worked in during his thirty years in Knoxville stands; the last was torn down when the Andrew Johnson Hotel was built in the 1920s. The jewelry shop Harris ran in the 1840s is long gone. Even Dr. Fouché's dental clinic on Gay Street was torn down in the 1990s.

But in 1869, six blocks due south of the Atkin House were the graves of a girl and boy George Harris once knew very well. The stones were then almost three decades old. Today, the graves of seven-year-old Harriet Josephine Harris and a toddler named George Harris remain there, maybe not quite as sharply legible as they had been the last time their father saw them.

# EASY, GENTLEMEN!

I t was early evening, the first chilly evening of the fall. "The nights are pinching cool now," as they said in 1871, down in the forties. People were still talking about the previous weekend's circus, the "Wild Tartarian Monster Yak," which had favored Knoxville with a visit, and "Old Emperor, the War Elephant," which had paraded down Gay Street that Saturday. But now farmers were preparing for the fair season opening next week—harvest-time exhibits along with some big-money horse races. Sentimentalists were looking forward to the smells of the chestnut vendors who would surely be here soon.

Defying some expectations that the heavily damaged city was "finished" after the war, Knoxville seemed to be recovering, even adorning itself with some of the trappings of a city. Swiss immigrant Peter Staub's elaborate Opera House was in the works, and down the street the Great New York Grocery advertised English breakfast tea, "Old Governor" Java Coffee, dried herring, "New York cheese" and Havana cigars.

At sunset, the full moon was hardly visible in a hazy sky. On Gay Street, a group of men, weary of discussing business, were ambling past the site of Staub's Opera House toward the St. Nicholas Saloon for a drink. Run by well-known saloonkeeper Nicholas Eifler, that popular establishment at the base of a hotel was the chief competition for its nearest neighbor, the Lamar House, just across Cumberland Avenue. The St. Nick was known for its fresh beer and Norfolk oysters, the latter shipped in several times a week on the trains.

The men might have noticed the saloon's ads in that afternoon's *Daily Press &* *Herald*. Playfully exaggerating local enthusiasm for its oysters, the St. Nick's ad counseled, "Take it easy, gentlemen! Take it easy!"

One of those gentlemen outside the St. Nicholas was forty-four-year-old General James H. Clanton, of Montgomery, Alabama. Clanton was a revered veteran of Shiloh, now a Democratic politician; in fact, he was chairman of the Democratic Executive Committee of Alabama. He was in Knoxville that evening as an attorney representing his home state in a railroad controversy.

The stocky general wore a cashmere suit, likely the envy of chilly pedestrians on the sidewalks that evening. He was conversing with a "dark-whiskered gentleman," prominent Knoxvillian A.S. Prosser, when Tomlinson Fort, an adversary in the railroad case, approached with a stranger with whom he had been walking arm in arm.

The stranger to Clanton was a younger man, a Union veteran named David Nelson. Though only twenty-six years old, Nelson was known in Knoxville as Colonel Nelson. Barely in his twenties at war's end, he had already been promoted to the rank of lieutenant colonel, as a member of General Gillem's staff. It may have helped his career that he was the son of one of the state's most respected men of law. His father was Tennessee Supreme Court justice T.A.R. Nelson, who had been one of President Johnson's attorneys during the impeachment trial three years earlier. Dave Nelson, an attorney himself and a sometime Republican politician, might have seemed a promising legacy. Friends described him as warm, generous and impulsive.

That Wednesday, Colonel Nelson had been drinking.

Perhaps naively, Mr. Fort—a former Confederate officer himself—introduced Nelson as a man who had "fought us" during the war. From that first handshake,

The Schubert Hotel, home of the St. Nicholas Saloon, site of the shooting of former Confederate general James Clanton in 1871, was in this building, later known as the Cumberland Hotel. The building was destroyed in a fatal fire in 1946. *Courtesy of Mark Heinz.*

Nelson and Clanton didn't hit it off. The men were strolling in the direction of the St. Nicholas when Nelson, hands jammed in his pockets, began speaking elliptically about "a certain place in the city" where he could show General Clanton "something good."

That is, if he was "not afraid to go." It's not clear what he was alluding to. The scariest place in town might have been the neighborhoods down near First Creek that were developing a reputation for gambling and prostitution.

"Do you think I'm afraid?" replied Clanton.

"I don't know whether you're afraid or not," said Nelson.

Nelson should have known that this wasn't something you said to a veteran of Shiloh. His hands clutching his cashmere lapels, Clanton stopped in the street and demanded to know what the younger man meant.

"Well, if you think I'm afraid, just try me," Clanton said. "Name your friend, time, place and distance, any time or any place."

Nelson replied, "This is as good a time and place as any."

The shouting drew attention. Judge C.F. Trigg happened to be staying in Room 10 at the Lamar House and watched the proceedings from his window. Nelson was agitated, perhaps not expecting a challenge to a formal duel. "Keep cool, Dave," Fort said, without effect.

Clanton responded, "Fort, step off the ground for your friend."

Fort refused.

Apparently panicked by this burly Alabama Confederate who had just challenged him to a duel, Nelson ran ahead to Eifler's saloon as Fort urged Clanton to keep walking. Nelson emerged with a double-barreled shotgun. Perhaps it was his own gun; perhaps it belonged to a saloonkeeper. Partly shielded by a beer barrel, Nelson steadied the gun against an awning for support.

Clanton, apparently familiar with the codes of gentlemanly conduct, asked Tomlinson to pace them apart for a proper duel. Tomlinson declined, estimating that Nelson was too drunk to duel. Clanton stood his ground. Nelson's gun went off.

Clanton drew a pistol and fired. He was still standing with his pistol raised in the air when Nelson fired his second barrel and hit his mark. Clanton crumpled slowly forward on the Gay Street pavement, doubled up on his hands and face. The first to reach him was a black boy, perhaps a servant. "Take my hat and pistol," Clanton said. "I have done all I can."

Nelson fled inside the St. Nicholas Saloon but escaped through a back door. He made his way to the family home on Cumberland Avenue, confessed to his father that he had shot a man and then slipped away. He left on a borrowed horse, just after sunset, riding west.

Gay Street in 1869, near the Lamar House, the approximate site of the Nelson-Clanton shooting two years later. Gay Street was reportedly paved in the 1850s but appears pretty dusty in this scene. The occasion of the photograph and the identity of the men standing in the street are unremembered. *Calvin McClung Historical Collection.*

Clanton's friends carried his bleeding body into a confectionary at the Lamar House. It was the same building where, not eight years earlier, another wounded general, a Union general named Sanders, had been brought to die. Doctors counted almost twenty wounds in the general's right side, at least fifteen of which had penetrated his chest, severing arteries and piercing a lung. They got some shot out of his back, but it was no use.

General Clanton's corpse lay in state at the Lamar House library, available, if briefly, for public viewing. It was the custom.

A block away, mortician L.C. Shepherd advertised that with the help of Taylor's Patent Corpse Preserver, "I am prepared to keep bodies from four to six days before putting them into coffins, when desired." Clanton's party didn't bother Shepherd. They carried his body straight down Gay Street to the Southern station for the midnight train to Alabama. An impromptu inquest that night at the Lamar House considered the murder of General Clanton.

Miles to the west, Sheriff Gossett pursued Nelson well into the chilly night. Out Kingston Pike, he encountered several witnesses, including an ailing liveryman who apparently knew Nelson. The man was so agitated upon hearing that he had helped a murderer flee that, moments after talking to the sheriff, he died. Nelson was last spotted several miles to the southwest, apparently on his way to Cleveland, where he had been living. At some point, he may have been passed by the night train to Alabama and General Clanton's corpse. Waiting for Clanton at home were a widow and six children.

Nelson reappeared in Knoxville two days later and turned himself in, pleading not guilty. He said that he had shot Clanton in self-defense. His famous father quit the state supreme court to help. After two years of delays, the trial focused on Clanton's violent nature. After deliberating, the jury read its surprise verdict: not guilty.

The whole state of Alabama cried foul. Some declared that the shooting was a political assassination and that Knoxville's justice system was implicated and corrupt. It was easy to believe that something was amiss in Knoxville; the city was, at the time, in the grip of a cholera epidemic. Judge T.A.R. Nelson died, unexpectedly, of the disease. David Nelson disappears from Knoxville records.

General Clanton became an Alabama martyr. Today, Clanton, Alabama, is a thriving town of eight thousand on the road from Montgomery to Birmingham.

# NIGHT SCHOOL

At the top of the masthead of today's *New York Times* is the line "Adolph S. Ochs. Publisher, 1896–1935." That unusual name has been there at the top of the box every day for more than a century. Adolph Ochs was the most influential publisher of America's best-known newspaper. It's possible that his name wouldn't be there, and that the *Times* as we know it wouldn't exist, if a teenager during the Reconstruction era hadn't been scared out of his wits by a graveyard in downtown Knoxville.

Kids had a lot of good reasons to be scared of the old Presbyterian churchyard. It was the final resting place of Professor Foster, who died young not long after his experiments with reanimating the corpses of hanged murderers had galvanized Knoxville in the 1820s. Governor, senator and fugitive William Blount's burial there in 1800 was rumored, as late as the 1860s, to have been a hoax, perhaps to allow him to escape federal charges of treason. U.S. senator Hugh Lawson White, known in Washington as "the Skeleton," ran for president in 1836, came down with the plague in 1838 and never fully recovered. He was buried here in 1840, and the minister employed to conduct his graveside service died in a fall from a horse before he arrived.

Then, during the Civil War, the Union army occupied this predominantly secessionist church, trampled old family plots and removed privacy fences. Toward the end of the war, the graveyard was the playground for a school for freed slaves. Beyond that, the banished congregation's elders complained that federals were permitting the graveyard to be used for unnamed "vile purposes."

First Presbyterian Church, as it appeared in the early twentieth century, with its much older graveyard. *Courtesy of Mark Heinz.*

It was in this disturbed state that young Adolph Ochs, son of Jewish Bavarian immigrants, first became acquainted with the graveyard on State Street. Even after the war, and after the graveyard had been cleaned up by the returning congregation, it was still a cause for dread to southern kids, who believed that these graves opened at midnight.

It had been known for decades as "the old graveyard." Decisively closed to new burials in the 1850s, just after another plague, the plot was too crowded to allow many exceptions to the rule. One such exception was probably the single reason a boy would fear this graveyard. His name was Abner Baker—"Mister Abner," as the fearful denizens of the riverfront would call him for generations to come.

If you've been out to that restaurant in the old brick house at Kingston Pike and Peters Road, you've probably heard some version of the story. Abner Baker, who once lived in that house, was a young Confederate, barely twenty-two years old, a small man with delicate features, once described as having a "manly bearing" but "modest and gentle as a girl." Baker returned from service in the war in 1865 to find that his father, Harvey Baker, had been murdered in his home.

One Monday in September, Baker rode into town, and at the courthouse he encountered a young clerk named Will Hall, a Union veteran who had been drinking in a saloon across the street. The two had words; no one knows what

32

The graveyard of First Presbyterian Church, as it appears today. Fear of Knoxville's oldest graveyard may have inspired a major career in American journalism. *Photo by the author.*

they were because within hours they both were dead. For reasons unknown, Hall began throttling Baker with his cane until it broke and then kept throttling some more. Baker drew a pistol and shot Hall in the head.

On the spot, Sheriff Marcus DeLafayette Bearden arrested Baker for murder and put him in the jailhouse on Hill Avenue. At dusk, a mob of one thousand citizens overwhelmed the jailhouse staff and yanked Abner Baker out of his cell. As the diminutive Baker called them a "pack of cowards," the mob hanged him from a tree on the hillside overlooking the riverfront. As downtown business commenced on Tuesday, Abner Baker's body was still suspended there, over the intersection of Hill and Walnut.

When his friends finally cut Abner Baker down, they needed a place to put him. There were a couple of graveyards downtown in those days. One was closed to new burials and the other was full of Unionists, including General Sanders. Abner's uncle, William, was an elder at the First Presbyterian Church and had some pull. William Baker was, in fact, a famous surgeon, known for assisting in one of the first successful hysterectomies in medical history. Perhaps with Dr. Baker's persuasion, the church's leadership decided to permit one more burial in that ancient, crowded graveyard.

To mark his grave, they chose an obelisk, symbolically broken at the top to represent a life, and maybe a mission, not completed. Even with the break, it's barely the tallest monument in the graveyard. "A Martyr for Manliness," the inscription reads. "His death was an honor to himself but an everlasting disgrace to his enemies."

His commemoration wasn't necessarily the last we heard of Abner Baker. For decades afterward, downtowners got used to the story that fishermen and river people climbed up the bank to tell: that last night, about midnight, they looked up the slope at that old tree on Hill Avenue, and there was Mr. Abner, still swinging in the night air.

Knoxvillians didn't believe them, of course. Those were superstitious people down in those riverside shacks. Heck, it could have been something else. A big possum, or something. That's what they kept seeing hanging from Abner's tree at midnight.

***

There's no doubt that a young Jewish kid, living just down the hill on Central Avenue where rainwater from the graveyard drained into First Creek, knew those stories by heart. Knoxvillians called the boy "Muley," sort of a joke, because his last name sounded like Ox. Muley Ox. Some in the family pronounced it Oaks, closer to the original Bavarian way, but Muley seems to have kept the short *o* pronunciation.

Both of Muley's parents were Bavarian immigrants who moved to Knoxville in the 1850s but then rode out the Civil War in Cincinnati, where Adolph was born. The war nearly split the family. Julius was a diehard abolitionist and Unionist who served for part of the war as an officer. His wife, Bertha, who had waved a bloody flag during the Bavarian revolts of 1848, had Mississippi planters in her family and was a Confederate. In Cincinnati, she smuggled medical supplies to the Confederates across the bridge in Kentucky in a baby carriage.

Toward the end of the war, they all moved back to Knoxville. They were a noisy, happy and, only briefly, wealthy family, until the Panic of 1867 ruined them. They had to give up their Sharp's Ridge chateau, known as Ochsenburg, to move into a shotgun house on Water Street, later known as Crozier Street and, later still, Central, a densely populated street alongside First Creek, known for poverty and, eventually, vice.

To supplement their father's income, the Ochs kids—Adolph first and then his brothers—took jobs with the only Republican, pro-Reconstruction newspaper in the South: Parson Brownlow's *Whig*. Adolph's favorite customer was eccentric Catholic

Young newspaperman Adolph Ochs (1858–1935) at about the time he was working as an apprentice printer for the *Knoxville Chronicle*. When he was only nineteen, he bought the *Chattanooga Times*; he later bought another paper with a similar name in New York and made it an icon. *Collection of the author.*

A Union veteran, William Rule (1839–1928) was a newspaper editor known in Knoxville as a mayor and postmaster, but his greatest influence may have been on a young admirer who worked for him as an apprentice, the future publisher of the *New York Times*. Throughout his career as publisher, Adolph Ochs kept a letter of introduction from Rule framed on his office wall. *Calvin McClung Historical Collection.*

priest Father Ryan—the famous Poet-Priest of the Confederacy, the strange young man with long, dirty hair, a murderous look in his eye and a knack for sentimental rhymes. Ryan was a mortal enemy of Adolph's employer and most of his own father's political associates, but he was also Adolph's best-tipping customer.

Young Ochs impressed Captain William Rule, the paper's editor after Brownlow became Reconstruction governor of Tennessee. Rule eventually led another Republican paper, a political successor to the *Whig*, the *Knoxville Chronicle*. Rule offered Adolph a job as an apprentice typesetter—a "printer's devil," as they called them in those days. It was a morning paper, and his shift was over at midnight.

The *Chronicle*'s office was on Market Square. To walk home when his shift ended, Ochs would have had to walk past the Presbyterian graveyard. Even if he skirted it by a couple of blocks—went down Union, say—from the corner of his eye he would still see the pale light reflected from the weathered marble in the graveyard, the solemn, meaningful slabs. What would he do if he saw something move—maybe over near Mr. Abner's tall obelisk? What would he do then, still more than a block from home?

"Can I stay tonight, Captain Rule?" he would ask, and he often did. Given a choice between walking past the Presbyterian graveyard at midnight and spending overtime hours learning the newspaper business, Adolph Ochs tended to choose the latter. He became an expert typesetter and learned nearly every other job a newspaper has to offer.

# This Obscure Prismatic City

By the time Adolph Ochs was nineteen, he was so confident of his late-night education in journalism that he figured he could run his own paper. Knoxville was overloaded with newspapers and newspapermen, though, and Adolph gathered that to move up, he might have to move. The year Parson Brownlow died, the Knoxville printers, who now called Ochs "Oxie," threw him a going-away party, and he moved to Chattanooga and helped revive a failing newspaper called the *Chattanooga Times*. He returned frequently to his hometown, sometimes serving as the *Times*'s Knoxville correspondent.

In 1896, Ochs came up with a phrase of his own, "All the News that's Fit to Print," and used it to advertise a small daily paper he had just bought in New York. The story goes that Ochs borrowed that phrase from his cousins, the Blaufelds, who ran a tobacco shop and tempted Gay Street pedestrians with the phrase, "All the Segars that Are Fit to Smoke."

Ochs created the *Times* as we know it today. The magazine, the book review and a famous reputation for fairness were among Ochs's contributions to what would become known as America's most important daily paper. He established Times Square in honor of his paper and, incidentally, the annual New Year's Eve party there. The electric-light ball drop was his idea in 1904.

For almost forty years, he kept, in his office, a framed letter of recommendation from Captain Rule back in Knoxville. Ochs was known to roam around the Times building and repeatedly astonished technicians in the typesetting room with his handiness with type. Unlike many publishers, he always knew exactly what his employees were doing.

Was that one graveyard spooky enough to inspire the founding of the most durable newspaper dynasty in America? "Perhaps the cemetery had something to do with it," wrote Ochs biographer Gerald Johnson in 1946. "If ghosts could inspire resolution in a fainthearted Prince of Denmark, why not in a stouthearted proletarian in Tennessee?"

As publisher of the *New York Times*, Adolph Ochs often returned to Knoxville, which he always pleased his audiences to call his favorite spot on the planet, to pay tribute to his "guide, philosopher, and friend," William Rule. The last time was shortly after Rule's death. Captain Rule died in 1928—of appendicitis, at the age of eighty-nine—when he was still editor of the *Knoxville Journal*, Republican descendant of the *Chronicle*.

Ochs was in his seventies when the *Journal* tried to get a sentimental shot of him when he visited Rule's grave at Old Gray on Broadway. Ochs politely waved the photographer away. Sorry, no, he said. See, he had always had this thing about graveyards.

# THE BATTLE OF DEPOT STREET

Y ou don't hear much about Depot Street anymore, but it's still there, across the freight yards from the Old City, on the northern fringe of what people think of as downtown. Near Gay Street it runs by the old Southern station and the parking lot of Knoxville's oldest restaurant. But Regas prefers to say it's on North Gay. You may never have heard of Depot Street, even if you've been on it a hundred times. It keeps a low profile, and the couple of blocks just west of Gay, where Depot takes an odd forty-five-degree turn to intersect with Broadway, make up one of the quietest sections of asphalt downtown.

On a late-winter Monday morning, you might walk down the middle of Depot and not worry too much about encountering anybody at all. On another Monday, in 1897, two thousand Knoxville men, black and white, were fighting for the right to be here. Some had shovels, some had fire hoses, some had guns, some had warrants. It was this little bent elbow of Depot for which Knoxville's best and brightest risked their reputations as reasonable men, and for which one gave his life.

The story opened almost eight years earlier, when a green kid named William Gibbs McAdoo mortgaged his future to buy Knoxville's mule-drawn streetcar system. Then only twenty-five, McAdoo was a successful attorney who had already been president of a couple of small businesses. Born in Georgia during the war, the son of impractically intellectual parents who taught history and wrote poetry, McAdoo had moved with them to Knoxville as a teenager in the 1870s, already frustrated with his parents' sacrifices. His father was much respected in Knoxville, but the younger McAdoo wanted to do something grander with his

In his astonishing career, William G. McAdoo (1863–1941) was a planner of New York subways, U.S. secretary of the treasury, first chairman of the Federal Reserve Board, U.S. senator from California and cofounder of United Artists. In 1897, he was in jail in his hometown of Knoxville for inciting a peculiar riot. *Courtesy of the Library of Congress.*

life. He dropped out of the University of Tennessee, where his father taught, and passed the bar anyway. After a spell working in Chattanooga, McAdoo returned home with a public-transportation idea so ambitious that conservative Knoxville investors balked. Undaunted, McAdoo found an investor named J. Simpson Africa, a Pennsylvania politician, banker and engineer. With Africa's help, in 1889, McAdoo bought Knoxville's mule-drawn streetcar system, expanded it and electrified it. Here, McAdoo built one of the South's first electric streetcar systems. The Knoxville Street Railway opened in 1890 with a grand electric trip down Magnolia to Chilhowee Park, amid loud hurrahs for the kid with the big idea.

As it turned out, though, McAdoo's equipment wasn't up to the strain of the industry still in its infancy. The electric streetcars broke down even more often than the mules had. Within two years, McAdoo's wonderful electric streetcar line was bankrupt. McAdoo wasn't thirty yet, but he had already suffered a business loss of a scale that might have impressed Wall Street.

Desperate for income, McAdoo moved to New York, settling his Tennessee family in an apartment on Eighty-seventh Street while he went to work as

A sketch of the 400 and 500 blocks of Gay Street around 1890, the year Knoxville began laying tracks for electric streetcars. Most of the buildings in this image were destroyed in the catastrophic fire of 1897 but were quickly rebuilt. The steeple in the background is that of the old First Baptist Church, demolished in the 1920s. *From an 1891 promotional brochure.*

an attorney. Back in Knoxville, a hard-nosed Ohio opportunist named C.C. Howell took over McAdoo's electric streetcar system and somehow made it work. McAdoo was doing well enough in New York but rankled at the idea of a Yankee interloper taking his place in his hometown. He was making a name for himself in the big city, but in 1896, he came back here in an attempt to defend his turf and redeem his fiasco.

# This Obscure Prismatic City

Market Square, looking north from above Union Avenue, as it appeared around 1890. The Knoxville institution, established before the Civil War, was long known as a place where a shopper could buy anything, from local produce to exotic imports. Perhaps the only place in town well known to all classes, genders and races, in 1900 it inspired a reporter to call it "the most democratic place on earth." *Drawing from an 1891 promotional brochure.*

Though business competition is often described as cutthroat, it rarely results in actual combat. In 1897, it did.

McAdoo bought part of his old streetcar route, including the steam "dummy" line from downtown to Fountain City, and began building new tracks on streets where no streetcar had run before. The new company, democratically known as the Citizens Street Railway, was a direct challenge to the other company that McAdoo had founded. Howell made things as difficult for McAdoo as possible, refusing to allow any access to McAdoo's old streetcar lines—especially at crucial Depot Street, which linked Broadway to the Southern terminal, then the city's main train station.

McAdoo's work crew of two hundred men were previously unemployed laborers who were grateful for the work. At their boss's instruction, they arrived at Depot Street long before dawn, with wagonloads of shovels and picks. By 5:30 a.m., witnesses noticed the men tearing up the pavement of the public street. Howell's associates heard the noise and called the cops. Three Knoxville policemen arrived and charged the crew with violating an obscure ordinance about digging up city streets during the cooler months. Theoretically, all two hundred laborers were under arrest. They outnumbered the police, who hauled a few workers away as the others proceeded with their work. Among the laborers were black gandy dancers, who sang work songs as they installed a pirate streetcar line.

Meanwhile, still before dawn, McAdoo representatives approached a judge, who found reason to believe that maybe these men did have the right to tear up Depot Street; he judged that it was inappropriate to arrest them for doing so. With a warrant in hand, Knox County deputies arrived at Depot Street to arrest Knoxville policemen for arresting honest laborers.

Back and forth it went as the sun came up on a very strange day. More than one thousand spectators accumulated during the early morning; an estimated eight hundred of them were sympathetic with McAdoo's two hundred workers. By 7:00 a.m., a wagon with railroad ties had arrived. The police chief himself was on the scene; he arrested McAdoo's foreman but failed to halt the work. Frustrated police rang the rarely heard Riot Alarm—four rings of the big bell in its tower on Market Square—calling every policeman in town to quell the riot. When a platoon of helmeted policemen arrived on Depot Street, they were met with plenty of county deputies to arrest them, too. At one time that morning, the police chief and the mayor of Knoxville were, theoretically, under arrest.

Finally, the Knoxville Fire Department arrived and took them all by surprise. Firemen set up hoses at either end of Depot, opened the spigots and accomplished

The Southern Railway depot early in the twentieth century. West Depot Street, site of the riot of 1897, is in the background to the left. *Courtesy of Mark Heinz.*

what the policemen had failed to do. They cleared crowded Depot Street with twin blasts of city water.

According to one reporter, "Frantic men, angry laborers, vociferous sympathizers, innocent onlookers, and helpless women and children all made a wild rush…to escape the bath that was about to be enforced on them."

It wasn't over yet. Frustrated laborers, many of whom hadn't worked in months, attacked the firemen with bricks. One black laborer attempted to cut an offending fire hose with a knife. As the fire chief attempted to prevent him, one of the older workers, another black man named Will Arnold, attacked the fire chief with a pick handle, knocking him senseless. Arnold then swung at a policeman, who shot him twice.

As Arnold lay dying, the huge crowd shouted, "Cold-Blooded Murder!" and "Hang the Police!" and "Hurrah for McAdoo!" Several others were injured in what the *New York Times* headlined a "SMALL RIOT IN KNOXVILLE."

Sam Heiskell, the young first-term mayor of Knoxville facing his first major crisis, appeared on Depot Street, appealing for calm. He climbed up on a fence at the elbow of Depot Street and pleaded, "In behalf of law and order, I ask and appeal to you to disperse! Go to your homes and let the matter be settled in the courts!"

Knoxville was one of the first southern cities to get modern electric streetcar service, though it came with a series of problems and caused at least one riot. This early postcard photograph of an electric streetcar dates from not long after William Gibbs McAdoo's adventures with the new technology. *Courtesy of Mark Heinz.*

An early twentieth-century cigar store.

The mob hooted Mayor Heiskell off the fence. The contractor told his men to go back to work. McAdoo himself, who had been arrested and detained in the city jail on Market Square before making bail, returned to the scene, proudly surveying his intrepid warrior-laborers' progress in laying railroad ties on what had been, a few hours ago, an intact city street. The young attorney stepped up onto a stone wall across Depot from where the mayor had spoken. "We have commenced this work, and propose to continue it until it is finished," he said, as the crowd cheered.

Wagons arrived carrying the rails to fasten to the ties already in place. Sheriff Groner spoke, declaring that he would arrest anyone who interfered: "It matters not who he might be." The mayor and police chief couldn't have missed the hint. Both were already under arrest. But at the courthouse, Mayor/suspect Heiskell conferred with another judge, obtaining an injunction to stop the work. This time, the sheriff couldn't argue. At 10:30 a.m., bereft of official allies, the workers finally laid down their tools.

In the first of his many trials by fire, Mayor Heiskell eventually prevailed. In a lawsuit, McAdoo eventually lost control of all his streetcar interests in Knoxville. Both of the lines that McAdoo had started were consolidated under Howell's guidance. As a legacy of capitalism at its most warlike, Knoxville inherited one of the South's finest public transit systems.

McAdoo returned to New York, and the rest of his career was more surprising than anything that happened on that day in February 1897. Four years after the Battle of Depot Street, McAdoo headed up the successful effort to build the first subway tunnel underneath New York's Hudson River, apparently without inciting any riots. Twenty years after he was arrested in downtown Knoxville, William Gibbs McAdoo was U.S. secretary of the treasury and, as cofounder of the nation's Federal Reserve system, its first chairman. Later still, McAdoo was U.S. senator from California and twice a strong contender for the U.S. presidency; some historians count him among the most qualified candidates ever denied that office. And while in California, he befriended some actors named Chaplin, Fairbanks and Pickford and was instrumental in founding a new studio called United Artists. He had always had a flair for the dramatic.

McAdoo's memoirs, aptly titled *Crowded Years*, are remarkably forthright about many of his failings—but they mention nothing about the Battle of Depot Street or the man who died for a streetcar track that was never finished. McAdoo did describe the failure of his original streetcar line, however, and suggested that the magnitude of his failure in Knoxville made unusual success on a national scale not only urgently desirable but necessary.

# TERROR ON THE WIRE

That winter, Knoxville was drawing tourists with what was billed as a "unique attraction," a miracle of Gilded Age technology thought to be the only one of its kind in the nation. Thanks to this marvel, Knoxville suffered a unique sort of tragedy.

That Saturday night in early February 1894 had seen an impressive turnout at Staub's Theater for Madame Rhea, starring in a production of Victor Hugo's *La Gioconda*. Perhaps like Cher, the actress's single, one-syllable name was famous. But today, Madame Rhea isn't as well known as her supporting actor that night: twenty-three-year-old William S. Hart, who, years later, would be one of Hollywood's first superstars. On Gay Street that night he didn't play the cowboy hero he later made famous in the silents. At Staub's, he was the hunchback Homodei. The place was packed.

The following afternoon, as thousands of Knoxvillians returned from church, it was unseasonably warm, a hint of spring. To many of them, it seemed a fine day for an afternoon outing. The riverbank near the university had been cleaned up after the Whittle sawmill explosion a few weeks before (a boiler had blown, killing four, including owner J.M. Whittle, hurling debris and parts of bodies up and down the riverbank). There, near where the mill used to be, as if to erase the memory, was a remarkable sight that Knoxvillians would never get used to seeing on their river. Two cables stretched from the north bank all the way to the top of Cherokee Bluffs to the south, a distance of several hundred feet. A trolley car suspended from those cables glided smoothly back and forth through the thin air all the way to the top of the bluffs, two hundred feet above the surface of the swift current of the undammed river.

Those cliffs were then still known as Longstreet's Heights. Only a handful of the older folks remembered the siege. Knoxville, which had more than quintupled in size since the war, was a dynamic industrial city of mostly young newcomers. But a few graying Knoxvillians could remember when the Confederate general's artillery man, Porter Alexander, had placed his cannons on that bluff and rained fire on the city.

But that was thirty years ago, a little more than that, in fact. By the 1890s, young folks were making fun of old-timers' preoccupation with that war. This was a peaceful Sunday afternoon, a time for modern diversions. The cable car was ferrying people up to the top of the bluff, where the city was planning a lofty public park, sure to be the envy of other cities not so forward-looking as Knoxville.

On the town end of the cables was a crowd of Knoxvillians waiting for their turns for a ride. Everyone had been assured that it was absolutely safe. After all, just weeks ago, the owners had hoisted five tons of sand in the car all the way to the top to prove it. It had been written up in detail in that technologically progressive magazine *Scientific American*.

An extremely rare photograph of the aerial cable car, an unusual amenity in 1894 Knoxville until a fatal accident, blamed on sabotage, scuttled it. It crossed the river to the heights on the south side, where a major park was planned. *Calvin McClung Historical Collection.*

Just after 3:00 p.m., six men, a woman and a teenage boy got into the gondola together. The machine's engines started, and it moved smoothly on its thirty-degree trajectory upward, higher and higher above the moving water's surface. No citizens had ever enjoyed such a perspective on their hometown as those who got to see it from the cable car. The snaky curves of the broad river were never so noticeable on the ground. The stately college on the Hill was visible as they climbed, as was, over to the left, old earthen Fort Sanders, now surrounded by modern houses. Off in the distance to the right were the five- and six-story reddish brown buildings of downtown. Ahead were the nearing rock walls of the limestone bluffs.

Two car lengths from the top, the passengers were looking forward to climbing out, perhaps with some curiosity about this new park and perhaps with some relief.

But then they heard a snap. By some accounts, which would puzzle investigators in days to come, there was also an explosion of some sort. But there was at least a snap, and the car slid rapidly backward, back out over the water, much faster than it had climbed, and gaining speed.

The operator, whose name was T.C. Lewis, clamped on the cable brakes, but they had little effect. "Like a flash the heavy car shot down the incline," reported the *Knoxville Tribune*. "There was a shriek from the brake shoes as they spun along the cable and two bright blue flames shot upward and sped along the cables as the car flew downwards." The pulling wire had broken, and "with the hiss of a monster serpent" it snaked wildly around the plummeting car. Then, "like a whip wielded by a Titan," the broken cable crashed into the car itself, finally tangling it in its own supporting cables. The car's high-speed slide halted all too quickly, dumping its passengers in a heap in the lower end of the car. They dangled 135 feet above the cold river.

Seven passengers, most of them painfully hurt, tried to rise on the slanted floor. One didn't. Young Knoxville attorney Oliver Ledgerwood lay on the floor of the car, almost still, with a deep gash in his head. For an hour and a half he lay there, as the others waited in their car, high above the river. There was no advice for such a problem. No one had been in that situation before in history, stuck in the air between two shores of a river.

Finally, workers succeeded in sliding a rope down to the victims of the unique aerial wreck. But that was hardly a solution until an impressive-sounding boat, a "steam yacht" called the *Vollet*, maneuvered itself below the entangled cable car. One by one, in a makeshift rope sling, the survivors lowered themselves to the deck of the *Vollet*. The sixteen-year-old boy went first, followed by the woman and then the others. Even passenger "George M. Phillips' corpulent form" came down safely.

The unconscious Ledgerwood remained. On the yacht, a black man named Andy Harris volunteered to climb up to the crippled car and carry Ledgerwood down. He hoisted himself the twenty-two fathoms above the river, got a grip on Ledgerwood and shouted down to the ship: "Let 'er go, lively!" As the *Tribune* recounted, "The negro hugged his bleeding burden to his breast" as he rappelled down to the deck.

It was just after 6:00 p.m. when the *Vollet* heeled toward downtown Knoxville, a doctor tending to Ledgerwood in a probably futile effort to make his last minutes comfortable. "His gasping denoted the approaching victory of death," reported the *Tribune*. As the boat approached the Prince Street wharf, it was almost dark. The doctor assessed his patient, his face visible in the flicker of the boiler's furnace. "Except for the bloody splotches it was deathly pale. Dr. Price took the man's hand and put his ear to his bloodstained breast. It was still."

There followed days and weeks of rumors of foul play, some of them circling around Ledgerwood's Sunday-afternoon date. His young female companion, who sat next to him in the gondola, was the only one uninjured in the wreck. When the broken cord was recovered and examined, it did indeed appear to have been cut deliberately, perhaps with a chisel. And there were numerous reports of an "explosion." Some wanted to blame that on the teenager, who many thought might have brought along a dynamite cartridge to drop into the water "for the fun of the thing," only to have it misfire. He and everyone else in the car denied knowing anything about what had caused the bizarre accident.

The only argument against the sabotage theory, according to the *Tribune*, was "the improbability of there being a fiend in existence diabolical enough."

A hasty inquest ascribed blame to the cable car company—not for defective equipment but for carelessness about guarding the apparatus from saboteurs.

"It is supposed," the *Tribune* concluded, "that Knoxville's unique attraction, the suspended cable railway, will now be relegated to the limbo of the past. It was at best only an experiment, but as is usual with such enterprises, its record is written in blood."

# THE FORGOTTEN DIRECTOR

Clarence Brown is a familiar name in Knoxville. Most know him as a well-dressed old man with a genial smile in a big painting in the lobby of the practical and well-equipped theater that bears his name. At a glance, most visitors to the Clarence Brown Theater on campus likely assume that he was a local philanthropist, a retired insurance executive, maybe, who sought immortality through an endowment big enough to earn the coveted reward of a name on a permanent building.

Fans of Hollywood's golden age, however, may think of Brown with regard to their own enthusiasms, as the MGM director of family blockbusters like *National Velvet* and *The Yearling*; as the dutiful studio-system director who helped nurture the early careers of Joan Crawford, Clark Gable and Greta Garbo; or as one of the most daring artists of the silent era. He is, today, the subject of at least two book projects by scholars in Europe.

His life and career are full of surprises and puzzles. He was a hardcore conservative whose sound-era masterpiece was too racially provocative for the Hollywood establishment. His most popular films are family movies, but his own family life is obscure: his own child, his child's mother, their identities and their fates are unknown, unmentioned in most profiles. Various acquaintances describing his treatment of others have called him "warm" and "cold." After churning out an average of two movies a year for a quarter century, he quit, at the relatively young—for a director—age of sixty-two. He then turned his attention to airplanes, automobiles and real estate, avoided Hollywood and rarely even watched a movie for the remaining thirty-five years of his long life.

And the final paradox is that this man who spent most of his adult life between California and Europe, who had not lived in Tennessee since he was a teenager, should become the single most generous alumni donor in the University of Tennessee's history.

Photoplay Studios in London is an institution dedicated to research and preservation of old movies. The man who may be the world's greatest living authority on silent films keeps his office there. Kevin Brownlow has been a champion of the work of Clarence Brown since his landmark book about silent film, *The Parade's Gone By...*, published in 1968. In that book, Brownlow writes:

> *Clarence Brown is one of the great names of American motion pictures—one of the few whose mastery was undiminished by the arrival of sound...Brown was a brilliant technician, but he also had a warm feeling for people.*

Brownlow recently said that Clarence Brown "made me a devotee of American silent films." Over a period of several years in the 1960s and '70s, Brownlow spent many hours with the notoriously difficult Brown and never quite figured the man out.

In an unpublished essay, Brownlow talks about his early acquaintance with the director. In 1959, the British scholar ran across a then-forgotten silent called *The Goose Woman*; put off by the title but intrigued by the cast, he bought an eight-reel copy.

> *From the moment it comes on the screen, its credit titles tinted blue, I knew this was something special. This was astonishingly well done from every point of view. I noted the director's name—Clarence Brown—and the date, 1925. Here was a film which you would find in no book about the history of cinema, yet one which was put together with as much love and as much artistry as any of the so-called classics.*

At length, Brownlow arranged a meeting with the then seventy-five-year-old director. "Thickset and tough, he resembled an oil tycoon," Brownlow continued. "He was not a warm man, and it took a lot of effort to get him to talk." When Brown did talk, what he said was often off-putting, brusque and politically extreme with what sounds like Archie Bunker's sensitivity.

"As far as I was concerned," Brownlow wrote, "Brown was an enigma. A teddy bear of a man with liquid eyes, robust, stern of visage, inarticulate"—Brown notoriously had trouble with both spelling and pronunciation—"he has nevertheless produced the most intelligent, eloquent pictures." Expressing his consternation with Brown to another of Brown's associates brought Brownlow to an irony he has never been able to unknot. "The strangest thing, we agreed, was that none of the characteristic elements of Brown's pictures were evident in his personal relations."

Who was Clarence Brown? He seems to puzzle everybody. Born in Clinton, Massachusetts, in 1890, he grew up with industrious parents. His father was Larkin Brown, an ambitious loom repairman with Georgia roots; his mother was a weaver named Catherine Ann, originally of County Down, Ireland. He was an only child, a kid always small for his age who seemed to make up for his lack of stature with energy and a quick mind.

Around 1900, Larkin Brown was offered a supervisory job at one of the South's most progressive textile mills—Brookside, in Knoxville, Tennessee. The city was at its industrial height, a compact metropolis of about thirty-five thousand, growing perhaps a little too fast. It was a pragmatic city, a beehive of factory workers, lawyers and salesmen, proud of its network of electric streetcars but too busy to establish an art museum, a symphony or even an urban park.

The Browns were practical, too, and moved to a modest house on the north side of town, within easy walking distance of Brookside, on West Baxter. One of the few childhood memories the director would share in later years was the thrill of climbing up the interior of Brookside's 152-foot chimney with his dad as it was being built.

The Browns moved frequently, each time to a slightly bigger house higher on the hill, but they always lived within clear view of Brookside's famous chimney. A neighbor, Laura Fogelsong, took an interest in the bright little Brown kid. An insurance man's wife originally from Ohio, Fogelsong ran a school of dramatic

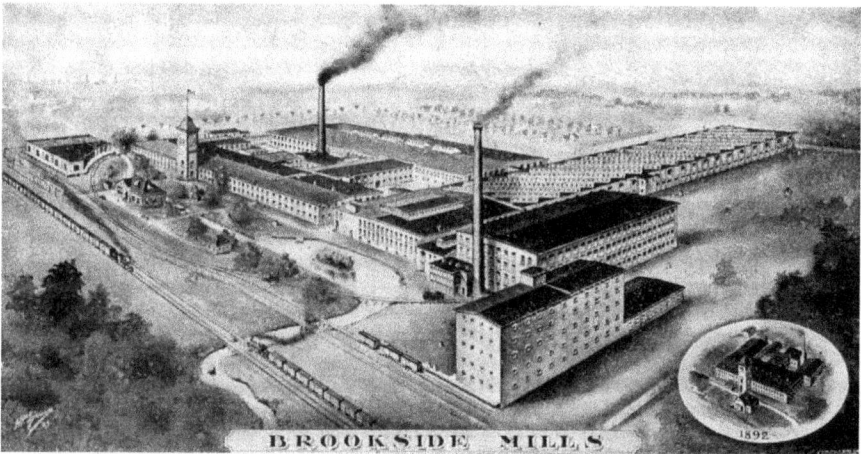

Brookside Mills, a major weaving mill on the north side of Knoxville, as it appeared when Clarence Brown's father went to work there. *From a 1904 promotional brochure.*

Diminutive Clarence Brown (center right) was only fifteen when he graduated from Knoxville High School. *Courtesy of University of Tennessee Archives.*

elocution and for a time kept a studio on Gay Street. Clarence Brown, small for his age, was her star pupil; he took lessons from her for seven years.

With Mrs. Fogelsong's encouragement, he became almost famous in early twentieth-century Knoxville for his recitations of poetry. A Memorial Day or Washington's Birthday celebration might include several musical selections, with a recitation from little Clarence Brown, a passage from Shakespeare, Longfellow or Poe, to liven it up a little. One gets the impression that people thought he was cute and also that maybe he didn't mind that.

He attended old Knoxville High (KHS); in the final years, it was located in an elaborately Victorian, castle-like building downtown at Union and Walnut. To get there, he probably rode the streetcar. Thirty years later, in one of his best-known films, *Ah, Wilderness!*, he would pay homage to KHS in ways that only KHS alumni would recognize. Though based on a Eugene O'Neill play ostensibly set in Connecticut and filmed near Brown's early childhood home in Massachusetts, the 1935 movie opens with a distinctive KHS banner, with Knoxville High's motto, *Ascendamus ad Summa*. Brown reportedly modeled classroom scenes on an old photograph of a Knoxville High classroom and added minor characters that reminded him of old classmates, including, reportedly, himself.

A female classmate later told a reporter that little Clarence was the class pet. "Oh, Clarence was a regular little runt. We just babied him to death—he was just like a little mascot. He was a very likeable kid, and bright, too."

Clarence Brown and some University of Tennessee classmates at a Knoxville-area swimming hole. The smallest student in every group, Brown was barely twenty when he graduated with two degrees. *Courtesy of University of Tennessee Archives.*

Brown loved the techno-futuristic Tom Swift books and all machines, especially automobiles. Cars and movies arrived in the American consciousness simultaneously. Both were rarities when the Browns arrived in Knoxville, and both were a common sight a decade later. By 1910, there were six movie theaters downtown.

By his own accounts, Brown wasn't interested in making movies until he was in his twenties—but he did show an early interest in the performing arts.

At Knoxville High, the precocious boy skipped a couple of grades. At age fifteen, he enjoyed a lively senior year as a member of the Musical Club, the Art Club and the Dramatic Club, in which he was part of a male minority of only six. In the Musical Club photo, he is one of the few students holding an instrument—a triangular-bodied mandolin.

The 1905 yearbook doesn't offer many details about his dramatic activities. At commencement exercises, held at the old Staub Theater on Gay Street, Clarence gave a recitation of "How the LaRue Stakes Were Lost," a once-familiar story. His interpretation was so popular that he gave an encore, closing the show with a humor piece. City councilmen were said to have been guffawing in the balcony. Classmates would later recall that he was the only senior who graduated in short pants.

The palatial Knoxville High School, originally known as the Girls High School. Located on Union Avenue at Walnut Street, it served as the city's main high school until the completion of a new building on the north side of downtown in 1910. Clarence Brown attended this school and reportedly based some of the sets and characterizations in his 1935 movie *Ah, Wilderness!* on his memories of it. *Drawing from an 1891 promotional brochure.*

Just one short block downhill from Knoxville High was O.C. Wiley's optical and photographic shop, which ran prominent advertisements in school publications. Among Wiley's employees was a talented young clerk, in his twenties when Brown was at Knoxville High. Jim Thompson would become twentieth-century Knoxville's best-known photographer and would make the city's first known motion pictures. Thompson's oldest surviving film is a short clip of a fire engine on old Commerce Street dating from 1915.

The Browns moved from one house to another but always within a stone's throw of North Central. Just a few blocks south on Central was the infamous Bowery, the district of saloons and whorehouses denounced by reformers. Saloons appear, sympathetically, in several Brown movies, and one might wonder whether he was working from memory.

Much of Brown's early life seems charmed—that of a spoiled only child living with supportive parents—but it had some dark moments. Years later, he would recall a trip to visit his Brown grandparents in Atlanta in 1906. He happened to be there, downtown, during the worst race riot in that city's history. He recalled white men beating up black men with bats and razors, leaving several dead. Four decades later, he would claim that memory as the inspiration for his boldest film.

The University of Tennessee (UT) was a tiny university confined to the top of the Hill. Brown enrolled as a diminutive fifteen-year-old. Fellow students called him "Brownie," which, given his stature, may have been inevitable. Though he seems to have avoided social fraternities, he instantly got involved in the Philomathesian Literary Society, an intellectual group that emphasized public appearances. His freshman year at the society, he held the title of "Declaimer." He represented the club in an "Intersociety Contest" and won.

The year he won those awards, sixteen-year-old Clarence rated a separate listing in the city directory, as a "student" boarding at his parents' West Scott address. Around 1908, they moved one block from there, across Central, to 121 East Scott, the house remembered today by Old North preservationists as the Clarence Brown home. Among their closest neighbors was a Swedish family named Sjoblom. It's probably too much to assume that this association had anything to do with Brown's unusual rapport with a certain Swedish actress almost twenty years later.

At UT, he majored in engineering, and after freshman year, he kept a lower profile. The prodigy who sped through high school may have struggled with college. Perhaps partly because he chose to double-major in electrical and mechanical engineering, he took an extra year.

Bachelor's candidates wrote theses in those days, and he didn't have to travel far to research his. His subject was the efficiency of the turbines at his dad's employer, Brookside Mills. "Economy and Power Distribution of Plant No. 2, Brookside Mills," is the dry name of his thesis, which includes hundreds of carefully recorded data. "By artfully attending to the firing of the Hawley furnaces," he concludes, "practically smokeless combustion can be obtained." What his dad, the superintendent, thought of the teenager's proposed improvements isn't recorded.

A major MGM director by the mid-1920s, Clarence Brown (1890–1987) poses with his Irish-born mother, who eventually left Knoxville to join him in California. *Courtesy of University of Tennessee Archives.*

56

The 1910 yearbook's profile of Brown suggests that those freshman triumphs with the Philomathesian Society composed the high point of his five years at UT. "He's a collegier, all right, for he's got a little college cap," goes a yearbook editor's odd summation. "Brownie early won fame as a declaimer, and carried off all the honors in his first year. After that, the society bee stung him, and since then it has been 'the ladies for mine' with him."

He dated one of UT president Brown Ayres's daughters. Most of the graduating seniors offered brief, pithy quotations to go with their profiles. Brown cited an obscure bit of romantic verse from the Roman poet Archias: "What, fly from love? Vain hope, there's no retreat / When he has wings and I have only feet."

He graduated with two engineering degrees as he turned twenty. He was, by then, full grown, topping out at five feet seven. He was last listed in the Knoxville directories in 1911, still living with his parents and working as a "traveling salesman."

After leaving town, he moved around some. As war broke out in Europe, Brown seemed to be settling in Birmingham, where he had set himself up as an automobile salesman and mechanic, a sporty profession in those days. As he would later tell it, a lunch break at a nickelodeon near his dealership convinced him that he should be making movies. In 1915, he set out for Fort Lee, New Jersey, the pre-Hollywood movie capital and the headquarters of Peerless Studios, determined to meet a director he had known only by name in some of the more artistic movies he'd seen—Maurice Tourneur. On his way, he stopped off in Knoxville and talked to his old mentor, Mrs. Fogelsong. According to her son's recollection, she thought it was a terrible idea. "She thought he was too fine a boy to get mixed up with the movies, and tried to persuade him not to case his lot with that type of people."

He went anyway and had some astonishing good luck. On a ferry, he heard that Tourneur was looking for an assistant director. Brown followed some movie people onto the location, and when the day's shoot was over, he pounced on Tourneur, one of the best-known motion picture directors in America.

As he later recalled the encounter to author Kevin Brownlow, "Brown told Tourneur he came to apply for the job. 'Who have you been working for?' Tourneur asked. 'Nobody,' Brown responded. 'I'm in the automobile business.'"

Tourneur was understandably skeptical, but Brown convinced him that his lack of experience was an asset. He asked, "Why don't you take a fresh brain that knows nothing about the business and bring him up your way?"

As Brown summed it up for Brownlow, fifty years later, "He fell for that argument." Brown and Tourneur worked closely, in a sort of yin-yang harmony. Tourneur was tempestuous and impractical; Brown, calm and businesslike. The engineer learned the business better than Tourneur ever did.

Brown's head wasn't always so level. Much of his early personal life remains obscure, but in 1917, he is known to have fathered a child. She went by the name Adrienne Brown. The identity of the mother, and whether the girl's parents were ever married, hasn't been proven. The girl is sometimes pictured with Brown on movie sets in the '20s, but the two apparently didn't live together long.

Brown took a break of a few months to enlist in the Army Air Corps, training pilots for combat in Europe. When he enlisted, at age twenty-seven, he listed his occupation as "director."

With Tourneur, he was more an assistant, or editor, but Brown is believed to have taken a strong hand in some of Tourneur's films, like the unusual special-effects fantasy, *The Blue Bird*. After Tourneur was injured and unable to finish it, Brown ended up directing much of the classic *Last of the Mohicans*. By then, they had moved to Hollywood, and Brown realized he could do this himself.

Brown split amicably with Tourneur and went to work for Universal, making several unusual silent features, like *The Signal Tower*, *The Goose Woman* and *The Eagle*, starring Rudolph Valentino as a stylishly vengeful Cossack. Part swashbuckler, part romantic melodrama, part sly screwball comedy, the 1925 silent was one of Valentino's last films and has a reputation as one of his best. Another early Brown film, *Smouldering Fires*, features a subject unusual at the time—a powerful middle-aged businesswoman who falls for a much younger employee. Brown's films of that era have a stark, vivid, artistic quality to them; some are almost like a series of carefully framed photographs at an exhibition. The lighting, many said then and continue to say now, was perfect.

By the mid-1920s, Brown had a reputation among the studio heads as one of the best directors in Hollywood. After a flirtation with Paramount, he befriended a rising producer named Louis B. Mayer and joined his project, an arrogant new film company called MGM.

Mayer, in his early forties and not quite six years older than Brown, had a reputation for being selfish, tyrannical, petty and generally unlovable, but for a quarter century, the two men would be close friends. Even as an old man, Brown wouldn't countenance any insinuation about Mayer's character. Kevin Brownlow admits that in his conversations with Brown, "I kept forgetting his friendship with Mayer, and made tactless remarks about the man." Brown always responded, "Louis B. Mayer was my closest friend in the picture business."

One of Brown's first jobs with MGM, a proposal he concocted with Irving Thalbert, was to take a Swedish actress little known in America, except for her reputation for impossibility, and put her in a movie with major star John Gilbert. Greta Garbo had never gotten along with an American director before she met

# This Obscure Prismatic City

Clarence Brown, whose patience and calm demeanor disarmed the famously temperamental actress.

Brown's Garbo-Gilbert vehicle, *Flesh and the Devil*, was a major hit of 1927. Brown directed Garbo in six major movies over the next ten years, including her first talkie, *Anna Christie*, in which she plays a former prostitute ("Gimme a viskey..."). The two, neither famous for their chumminess, would remain close friends for sixty years.

Brown learned to play the Hollywood game. For most of his career at MGM, he had a reputation as a "company man" and a practical problem solver, perhaps befitting a guy with two engineering degrees. (His career shift may seem surprising, but it had at least one precedent: the great Russian director Sergei Eisenstein also had studied engineering.) Sometimes Brown's technical inventiveness looks something like art. He was always finding ways to put cameras in unlikely places, especially to show motion. In a couple of movies, he uses trains to display a diversity of humanity and, in an unusual scene in the early Joan Crawford movie *Possessed*, a pageant of life's options.

The 1935 Garbo movie *Anna Karenina* features a technically difficult scene at a banquet: a camera travels backward down a long table, between place settings, slowly revealing the extent of the extravagant feast. Some shortsighted film historians have assumed that Brown purloined the technique from a von Sternberg movie made the year before. But as Irish scholar Gwenda Young notes, Brown had used an identical technique back in 1925 in *The Eagle*, a silent rarely seen until recently.

For years, Brown enjoyed a plush but almost random career piloting major MGM pictures—biopics, adventure films, costume dramas, light comedies and animal pictures—all made with Clarence Brown on the megaphone ordering around the biggest stars of the day: Garbo, Tracy, Gable, Crawford, Stewart. Most were monetarily successful, and six were nominated for the top Oscar. A few, if you heard the title, might ring a bell. But Brown was never strongly associated with one particular genre, which is one reason scholars believe he is not as widely recognized as some of his contemporaries, like Ford, Capra and Hitchcock.

With the 1944 success of *National Velvet*, starring child phenomenon Elizabeth Taylor, followed by *The Yearling*, famously starring a non-actor in the lead—Claude Jarman Jr., a kid Brown had scouted from a Nashville schoolroom—Brown could have developed a reputation for popular and well-made family movies about animals and children, as unlikely as that might have seemed a decade earlier, when he was making films about adultery and prostitution.

After his parents moved to Hollywood in the 1920s to enjoy their son's surprising success, Brown had little contact with Knoxville or Knoxvillians, except that he followed football. UT football was little more than a club sport when Brown attended, but by the 1930s, Coach Robert Neyland's Vols had become famous. When the astonishing 1939 Vols, unscored-upon in their regular season, came to Los Angeles to accept their first Rose Bowl bid in early 1940, Brown greeted them with an extravagant party at his ranch.

Late in his career, against a backdrop of national anxiety about racial segregation, MGM uncharacteristically chose to interpret a William Faulkner novel, *Intruder in the Dust*, a racially charged murder story that was, in several respects, a darker, sharper version of *To Kill a Mockingbird*, a novel not yet written. They got Brown, then in his late fifties and a rare southerner among Hollywood directors, to do the honors. It is an astonishing movie for 1949, or now, one that author Richard Wright declared was the only Hollywood movie black Americans could take seriously. Brown, who was also the movie's producer, later insisted that he had to talk MGM into letting him do it, and some of its notes of grim absurdity seem creditable to the director. Brown said it was his way of working out what he had seen in Atlanta in 1906.

Some thought it deserved the Oscar, and indeed it did win the British Academy's award for best picture that year. It was shut out of the American nominations.

Soon afterward, about the same time Louis B. Mayer retired, Clarence Brown gave it up. He wrapped *Plymouth Adventure*, starring Spencer Tracy and Gene Tierney, which won the Oscar for Best Effects, and quit making movies.

Brown was one of the very few who stayed in touch with the mysterious and reclusive Greta Garbo. Brown and his wife sometimes vacationed with Garbo in Europe. He played golf, flew planes, invested in real estate and drove sports cars. (Brownlow recalls riding around California with the seventy-five-year-old Brown gunning his white Mercedes to speeds of well over one hundred miles per hour.)

Brown claimed that he saw only two movies after 1952: *Dr. Zhivago* and *Born Free*. He liked them well enough, he said, but he didn't want to get sucked back into the business.

Meanwhile, back in 1960s Knoxville, UT's honchos were stirring up ideas for a fundraising project on the West Coast, where many alumni lived. UT president Andy Holt and fellow administrators Ed Boling and Charlie Brakebill would go to Los Angeles, host a dinner and invite everybody in show business they could think of with a Tennessee connection. The famous ones were Dinah Shore, Tennessee Ernie Ford, Polly Bergen and Patricia Neal. Many Knoxvillians were not old enough to remember Clarence Brown, and some UT big shots admitted that they'd hardly heard of him. He hadn't made a movie in more than fifteen years, and even before that, he had kept a low profile.

But a few of the older UT supporters recalled that the retired director had once been a big Vol fan. They put him on the list. If they had known more about Brown, and the fact that he rarely responded to invitations, they might not have bothered.

As it turned out, all of the familiar stars, the ones who sometimes made appearances at Neyland Stadium at halftime, were tied up and offered their regrets. The only ones who accepted were seventy-seven-year-old Clarence Brown and his wife, Marian, the former journalist he had married soon after the war. The UT chiefs reconsidered whether they should bother with the trip at all. "That's a fur piece to go for one couple," complained Andy Holt. But they went anyway and met an interesting guy.

At that first meeting, Brown was a sphinx. "He was a hard-nosed businessman," Brakebill later recalled. "He was a person it was not easy to get to know. But he said that what he learned at the school of engineering, his experience growing up…made his movie career possible."

Brown and Holt corresponded about a possible half-million-dollar endowment for a theater-arts center. At first it seemed clear that nothing would be coming soon. "We thought, well, we tried, we went to bat," said Brakebill. But within three months, they got word that Brown would pony up the cash. Some assume that his wife's persuasion had a lot to do with it.

Brown visited his hometown several times over the next six years. Brakebill and Boling drove him to the north side of town, where a couple of his old houses

Knoxville-raised MGM director Clarence Brown with one of his best-known actors. Greta Garbo, who appeared in six Brown films, called him her favorite director. *Courtesy of the Library of Congress.*

and the towering Brookside chimney were still standing. Brown reminisced about adolescent pranks, like greasing the trolley tracks on Cumberland Avenue, and upon seeing how UT had expanded so far beyond the Hill, he remembered old Circle Park, where his mother had learned to drive a buggy.

In May 1970, UT hosted an eightieth birthday party for Clarence Brown. The occasion happened to arrive with the worst student unrest in the university's history—a month of student strikes, vandalism and even firebombings. Days earlier, police had arrested scores of students when they loudly demonstrated against President Nixon's appearance at a Billy Graham crusade at Neyland Stadium. UT administrators were already nervous about how students would respond to Brown's conferences with administrators. In the midst of it all, the old man vanished from his room at the Sheraton on Cumberland Avenue.

As it turned out, he had just been curious. He strolled over to the student center to talk to the students demonstrating against the war. "I had a great visit," he said. "These students, their interest in protesting is not even skin deep."

A few months later, he returned to Knoxville again, to dedicate the new theater that would bear his name. It opened with a screening of *The Yearling*.

"He couldn't believe he was being honored that way," Ed Boling, who was then president of the university, said later. "He thought everybody had forgotten him. He thought people didn't realize who he was." Brown's wife remarked that his UT associations were "like a second life" for him.

Clarence Brown died in 1987 at the age of ninety-seven. When Marian Brown died six years later, she left half of the childless couple's estate to a home for Hollywood professionals in California and half to endow the Clarence Brown Theater program at UT—about $11 million in all.

The Browns also left UT their personal papers and artifacts, which are stored in dozens of bankers' boxes in the Hoskins Library's Special Collections. Included in those papers are hundreds of letters and photographs, documents like Brown's birth certificate and army papers, as well as oddities like ash trays personalized by Louis B. Mayer's wife, Lorena. It's a lush collection of a sort that usually ends up at a major film school.

Though the public library stocks many of his MGM classics, decades pass without a Clarence Brown film being shown in public in his hometown. His older movies, the silents that film critic James Agee considered his best, like *Smouldering Fires*, *The Signal Tower* and *The Goose Woman*—the film that convinced British film scholar Kevin Brownlow that Brown was a major talent—aren't available in any format.

Today, judging by the way Google listings stack up, the Clarence Brown Theater on the UT campus may be better known than Clarence Brown himself.

# THE MOAN

Early in the first year of what wasn't yet understood as the Great Depression, it seemed as if everything in Knoxville was going wrong. The newspapers were full of murders, robberies, prominent suicides. One businessman shot himself in his upscale Fort Sanders apartment. Another, whose downtown grocery was going into receivership, left work as if for lunch, drove out to Bearden and calmly walked into an oncoming train.

Late one cool night that March 1930, an explosion rocked Union Avenue and an apartment building burst into flames. Some people leapt out of second-floor windows onto the sidewalk. A family of three died in their apartment. The fire itself, one of the worst of its era, was also one of the strangest.

As firefighters battled the blaze, an enigmatic German razor grinder climbed to a second-floor landing down the alley, collapsed and stopped breathing.

Two weeks later, just on the other side of Market Square, a young black woman walked into a white people's hotel and sang a song into a recording machine as several technicians from up North listened on headphones. When she sang her song about that weird night on Union Avenue, it may have been the newest song in the world. She called it "The Arcade Building Moan."

The Arcade Building and the peculiar fire that destroyed it are nearly forgotten. Even local historians have been known to doubt that the building even existed. It's likely that no one alive remembers any of the people who died in the blaze. But a song about them still makes the rounds around the world.

This confluence of events would have been unlikely anywhere but in an American city—anywhere but in this particular American city.

St. James Hotel, Knoxville, Tenn.

The St. James Hotel, a modest but durable hotel on Wall Avenue, was the site of a brief but interesting series of country, jazz and blues recording sessions in 1929–30. *Postcard image courtesy of Mark Heinz.*

The St. James Hotel was on Wall Avenue, in the short block between Gay Street and Market Square. About thirty years old and constructed entirely of concrete, it was advertised as Knoxville's first "fireproof" building. It was an important distinction to claim in those days, a stone's throw away from the 400 block of Gay, which had recently suffered the worst fire in Knoxville history.

Most of the time the St. James was just a hotel, but for several months in 1929 and early 1930, it doubled as a recording studio for a national record label. The Brunswick Company had been known for decades for manufacturing pool tables, but in the 1920s, as Brunswick-Balke-Collender, it became known as the only record company big enough to challenge Victor. Its subsidiary, Vocalion, was known for popular records, especially blues, on 78 rpm shellac.

Popular music recording was still new in the 1920s. Tastes were shifting rapidly, and most of the new music in America—country, blues, gospel and jazz—was coming from certain regions in the South, especially New Orleans, the Mississippi Delta and the Southern Appalachians.

Recording companies like Vocalion were keen to catch the best talents before the competition did. Like *National Geographic* explorers, rival record companies set up recording sites in various locations and took in every interesting sound they could find.

In 1927, Victor went to Bristol, where that major label discovered the Carter Family and Jimmie Rogers—both would sell a lot of records in years to come and prove to be influential in the development of country and popular American music. In 1928, Columbia went to Johnson City, trying to match Victor's success.

In 1929, Brunswick/Vocalion gave Knoxville a try. The largest city in that series of trolling expeditions was appealing to the national record company perhaps because the area had some reputation as a center of the burgeoning country music market. Even before the landmark Bristol sessions of 1927, Knoxville country and folk musicians like Charlie Oaks, George Reneau and the duo Ted and Mac had found some success with records made in New York as early as 1924. Knoxville's Sterchi Brothers Furniture, a major marketer of phonographs in the South, sponsored many of the early New York recordings of iconic stars like Uncle Dave Macon.

The prospects of the promising "hillbilly" market might have drawn the record company's attention, but in Knoxville, Brunswick found a good deal more than country.

In the summer of 1929, several technicians from Brunswick's home office in Muskegon, Michigan, unloaded sixteen hundred pounds of recording equipment into the St. James Hotel. It seemed a good spot because near the lobby it already had a soundproof studio, fitted out by local radio station WNOX, which had been Knoxville's most popular radio station for about nine years. In those less-cluttered days, its signal was strong enough to reach across several state lines, and it already had a reputation for broadcasting live music.

The technicians who helped set up the studio are remembered, barely, as R. Chaff, H.C. Bradshaw and W.J. Brown. The guy in the booth was the musical director, Richard "Dick" Voynow, who some sources indicate was the one who prompted the Knoxville sessions. In jazz circles, Voynow was something of a celebrity; local musicians would likely have recognized his name. He had been pianist and leader of the original Wolverines, alongside legendary cornettist Bix Beiderbecke. In photos of that legendary band, Voynow appears as a dark, dapper fellow with a mustache and his hair parted in the middle and plastered down in the style of the day. It was reportedly a spat with Voynow that caused Beiderbecke to leave the Wolverines.

Voynow also collaborated with songwriter/pianist Hoagy Carmichael; the two shared credit for the radio hit "Riverboat Shuffle," which would be recorded by dozens of jazz bands. By 1929, Beiderbecke and Carmichael had become two of the biggest stars in jazz. Voynow, a competent pianist but perhaps not the celestial talent that some of his collaborators were, may have thought he had a better chance distinguishing himself as a producer.

Word about Voynow's project got around. Musicians came from all over to record at the hotel on Wall Avenue. During that period before Nashville had any reputation for music recording, musicians from across the region, including several from Middle Tennessee, traveled to Knoxville to make records at the St. James. Among them was Nashville's biggest star, Uncle Dave Macon.

Knoxville was, at the time, a crowded, noisy, exciting, grotesque, lively, filthy place of electric streetcars and belching smokestacks, of rednecks and sophisticados, in an uncomfortable transition between the booming urban city with metropolitan pretensions it had been at its Edwardian peak and an ordinary mill town, which at its worst seemed something like a giant refugee camp for the rural dispossessed. Some of the industry that had pushed Knoxville forward since Reconstruction was running out of steam, and the earnest progressive movement that promised to rebuild much of Knoxville in the 1920s seemed to be dying before it had fully bloomed. The most obvious green shoots in Knoxville were musical ones.

Brunswick already had a presence in town. Sterchi Brothers Furniture, then touted as the biggest furniture company in America, was headquartered on Gay Street. Sterchi was a big supporter of the booming recording industry. Sterchi's own Gus Nennstiel, an electronics expert, was an agent for Brunswick/Vocalion.

In Knoxville, Voynow and company found a kaleidoscope of styles and genres and, predictably, a good deal of lunacy.

During a period of several months, a variety of musicians—mostly male, mostly white—walked into the St. James. Uncle Dave Macon himself, the vaudevillian banjoist who became one of country music's first real stars, recorded there on March 31, 1930, with his son. Macon was already famous. A few, like the Sievers family band, the Tennessee Ramblers—featuring Willie Sievers, perhaps the first female guitarist to record in country music—would go on to moderate fame. Most of those Voynow recorded wouldn't fare so well. More than half of the bands recorded at the St. James were country bands, broadly defined; several of them worked in some slapstick humor. Many were talented, but the sensibility of many of the sessions is something along the lines of a barn warmer attended by the Three Stooges. You get the impression that for these months, the St. James was a jolly frat house party of spirited young musicians and would-be musicians.

A couple of early jazz orchestras recorded there, including Knoxville's biggest big band, Maynard Baird and his Southern Serenaders, representing their party standard, "Postage Stomp." Like most of the others, their selections were a sampling of up-tempo songs that they had been playing for years. Sixty-five years after it was recorded, the St. James recording of "Postage Stomp" wound up on a Yazoo CD compilation aptly called *Jazz the World Forgot.*

In an article that emphasized the project's "Hill-Billy Music" recordings, a *News-Sentinel* reporter added, "There was some Negro music, too." That polite footnote was perhaps an understatement.

The Tennessee Chocolate Drops, an unusual black string-jazz band featuring irrepressible fiddler/mandolinist Howard Armstrong, was one. They played their "Knox County Stomp" and another called "Vine Street Rag," named for the cultural spine of Knoxville's black community. By mistake, it was printed as "Vine Street Drag" on the label. The Chocolate Drops would later be better known as Martin, Bogan and Armstrong and were still recording and popularizing their eccentric version of the blues around the world as late as the 1970s. Their St. James recordings are part of the soundtrack of the Terry Zwigoff documentary, *Louie Bluie.*

And then there was Leola Manning.

This angular black woman with almost Mediterranean features was nothing like anybody else who walked into the lobby of the St. James. An East Knoxville

A rare photo of East Knoxville cafeteria worker Leola Manning, about the time she made some recordings at the St. James Hotel that would become well known among lovers of early jazz and blues only sixty years after she made them. *Courtesy of Tennessee Archive of Moving Image and Sound.*

cafeteria worker and aspiring evangelist of twenty-five, she was at the time struggling with a troubled marriage. A resident of East Vine Avenue, she was one of very few participating musicians who could have walked to her recording session at the St. James.

She recorded at the St. James near the beginning of Voynow's sessions, first on August 28, 1929, and then again the following spring, on April 4, 1930. Her work stands apart from the others, almost as if she was recording her songs in a different St. James, in a different era. It's purer, more earnest, more urgent and more startling.

The first couple of sides she cut at the St. James were religious songs done in a gutsy blues style that may have alarmed the devout. "He Cares for Me"—a slow, mournful number, with syncopated piano and guitar accompaniment— seems to describe the death of a child: "When the Lord called my baby, I could not keep from crying / I could see that she was sick, but I could not believe she was dying."

"He Fans Me" is livelier, with a visceral ragtime heart. Despite its religious theme, it might have sounded more at home in a nightclub than in a church.

They were memorable performances. When she came back to the St. James about seven months later with four new songs, Voynow and company put her on the schedule.

Some of the new songs were plaintive, distressed commentaries on current events in Knoxville during that first year of the Depression, and she sang them almost like a town crier. One, "Satan Is Busy in Knoxville," seems to detail real-life murders:

> *In nineteen and thirty, the beginning of the year, so many people was made sad*
> *When Franklin was out, earning his bread, no fear or troubles he had;*
> *He was driving in the sun along the road*
> *And a robber jumped on his running board*
> *Who murdered this man nobody knows*
> *But the Good Book says they've got to reap just what they sow.*
> *'Cause Satan is so busy in Knoxville, Tennessee.*

She continues with a grislier account:

> *Not many hours later, a colored woman her name was True*
> *She was found with her throat cut*
> *From ear to ear below the Mountain View School.*

# This Obscure Prismatic City

The Mountain View School was in East Knoxville, on Dandridge Avenue. Leola Manning knew it well; she worked there.

She wrote all of her songs herself. She never called any of her songs "blues." It was, to her, a bad word, an unchristian word. One of her songs, "The Blues Is All Wrong," is an up-tempo boogie-woogie number that could almost pass for early rock 'n' roll or swing. The lyrics sound a little defensive, perhaps reflecting a typical middle-class reaction to her music in 1930:

> *This song's all right, if you think it's wrong…*
> *It's got the blues tune, but the words are right…*

They all sound like blues. But unlike most blues songs, not one of Leola Manning's songs is a love song. In "Laying in the Graveyard," she seems to picture herself after death:

> *I wouldn't mind dying, but I have to lay dead so long…*
> *Good morning, dead man; Mother, how do you do?*
> *I've been so long in this world without you.*

The newest song in the April session was based on a tragedy in the neighborhood of the St. James. Topical songs describing the news of the day were not unusual in popular music. But one song may be kind of a superlative for its era. One of the recordings Leola Manning made that day described a catastrophe that had happened only fifteen days before her session.

As always, she was careful not to call it "blues." She called her new song "The Arcade Building Moan."

The Arcade Building was a zigzag block away from the St. James, on Union Avenue. The quickest way to get there would have been to walk the length of crowded Market Square, past the farm wagons in the broad alleys on either side of the Market House.

Mention the "Arcade Building" today, and people will assume that you're talking about the better-known building on Gay Street, the old Journal Arcade. Built in 1924, it was the handsome, modern, marble home to the morning paper; its interior held an architectural arcade with offices on either side. To confuse historians further, there was an earlier building called the Arcade Hotel, also on Gay.

The Arcade Building in the song was the least prominent of them all. Built around 1910, it was a modest but versatile two-story brick structure on Union between Market and Walnut, broader than it was tall. Photographs of it when it was not on fire are hard to come by. Originally, it housed small shops and offices in its lower floors—tailors, florists, novelty shops and piano parlors, perhaps in an arcade setting—and middle-class residences above. By 1930, though, the building was almost all residential and not doing very well at that. It had nineteen units, only ten of them occupied. Affluent residents had been leaving downtown for over twenty years. But by 1930, downtown was coming to seem more and more like a place for working-class residents, especially those who couldn't afford cars.

Still, it was impressive how much you could squeeze into one block in 1930. On that block of Union were apartment buildings like this—the 1904 Sprankle, almost next door, was the larger of the two—offices and lots of retail. In that regard, this particular block of Union had something of a theme that made it different from any other city block. It was home to a shoe store, a paint store, a cigar store, a cobbler, two restaurants, a Western Union office, a real-estate office, a plumbing and heating company, a bakery, the Union Milk & Grocery and a pool hall. But the 400 block of Union was also the go-to block for all things tonsorial: the same block hosted two barbershops, two beauty shops and two barber supply stores.

One of the barber supply stores was run by an immigrant named Carl Melcher. Born in Solingen, Germany, a city no bigger than Knoxville near Dusseldorf, he had served the German imperial government in Africa before moving to the United States shortly after the First World War. He had Cincinnati connections but spent most of his time in Knoxville. At age fifty-nine, Melcher and his wife, Helen, lived in the Virginia Apartments at the corner of Market and Cumberland. They may have led a lonely life; neither had relatives here, and neither spoke English well.

Melcher was known as an expert mechanic and was, by some accounts, the best razor grinder in town, a skill useful to barbers. He sold his own tonsorial supplies, mixing hair tonic himself from mineral water and perfume. He also had a reputation as a fire enthusiast, often chasing the sound of sirens around town, even in the middle of the night.

Some, including cobbler Joe Baddich, who ran his own shop next door to the barber supply store, didn't like Melcher much. Despite their proximity, the two men hadn't spoken to each other for two years. Despite Melcher's reputation for skill, Baddich suspected that he wasn't getting much business. The German was often seen standing out on the Union Avenue sidewalk, waiting for customers. That March, he had only twenty dollars in the bank.

Though some regarded him as "affable," Melcher struck some as an unhappy man. He had told some that he expected to move away from

Knoxville, back to Germany and the shaky Weimar democracy where the Nazis were rising to power.

On the evening of Thursday, March 20, Herr Melcher did several peculiar things. First, he cashed out his bank account, all twenty bucks of it. Then, he ordered a fifty-five-gallon drum of gasoline from Gulf Oil. It was late in arriving, and he telephoned in angry, opaque accents. When the truck finally did come down his alley, Melcher asked the driver to help install a spigot into the barrel.

At 8:00 p.m., Melcher walked into the Union Lunch. Despite its name, it was a three-meal restaurant, open well into the evening. He asked proprietor Jim Evras how late his place was open. Evras replied that he usually stayed open until about midnight.

Melcher returned to the restaurant two hours later with a cardboard box. He told Evras to keep it until someone—not necessarily Melcher himself—asked for it.

It had been chilly on previous evenings that March, but this night was warmer, well into the fifties—finally a hint of spring. The movie houses of Gay Street were showing some of the early talkies. *The Girl Said No!* was playing at the Tennessee. *The Sky Hawk* ("Laughing at Death / Thrilling the World") was at the Riviera. Some theaters were still showing silents, but the big houses advertised "All Talking."

By 2:00 a.m., the Wilkerson family was probably sound asleep. Sylvester Wilkerson, thirty-two, was a former army recruiter who had recently retired from duty at Fort Oglethorpe. He married a slightly older woman who already had a son, Arthur Sharp, who was sixteen. The three lived together in their apartment at the Arcade.

The Union Lunch had closed down for the evening. The 400 block of Union never completely went dark; there was always, at least, the operator at Western Union. On this particular night, it was C.H. Nesbitt. When the fire started, he thought the boiler had exploded.

He ran outside. The whole block glowed lurid red. Broken glass was everywhere. The Arcade Building, with Baddich's Shoe Store, Martinello's Beauty Parlor, Frazier's Barbershop and Melcher's place, was on fire.

The fire department was right there—nine engines, two ladder trucks and dozens of firemen all over the block. One after another, people leapt from the second floor of the Arcade. A woman jumped and was entangled in telephone lines. A man jumped and landed on a passerby, a middle-aged man with a foreign accent. One man lowered a rope and nonchalantly climbed down. A traveling salesman who was staying at the Arcade was obliged to explain his preparedness: "I've been carrying a rope in my suitcase for twenty-five years, waiting for something like this to happen."

In spite of the streams of water blasting it, the fire leapt around the block, sending cinders into the air, skipping over some buildings to bite into others. Much of the 500 block of Market caught fire, but the Arnstein stood almost unscathed.

By the time the sun rose on the smoking rubble, people were calling it the worst fire in twenty years. Everyone seemed to have escaped the Arcade Building in time, except for the Wilkerson-Sharp family. Their bodies were found in the ashes, charred and in pieces, identifiable only by dental work and supposition.

A fourth victim's fate was more peculiar. On the second story of the Schriver Building, a block away and hardly touched by the fire, lay a portly middle-aged man. His hands were scorched, as if he'd held a live wire. His face was charred "to a crisp." He turned out to be Carl Melcher.

Melcher became the mystery of the week, and details of the gasoline delivery and the mysterious package were soon spreading around town. Investigators found that the package Carl Melcher had left at the Union Lunch held incoherent clues: some razors and scissors, apparently left by customers to be sharpened; a checkbook and an account book for his barber supply business; and a couple of insurance policies, life and business. It seemed odd that he had kept them; they had expired months earlier.

Adding to the mystery was the fact that at about the time of the explosion, a man with a German accent had called a taxi from Kern's Bakery on Market Square, cursing impatiently. Melcher had lived hardly three blocks away. He had no known association with the building where he was found.

Two weeks later, Leola Manning was in the draped studio at the St. James Hotel, singing into a microphone with her accompanist as four technicians listened on the headphones:

> It was on one Thursday morning, March the twentieth day
> I think it was about two a.m., I believe I can firmly say
> The women and the children was screaming and crying
> Not only that, they was slowly dying.
> Oh listen, listen how the bell did ring
> When the Arcade Building burnt down.

It was a song she had written, arranged and presumably rehearsed with a pianist, all in the previous two weeks. The ringing bell may have been the Market House bell, which hung in its belfry a stone's throw from the St. James. Since the

1880s, it rang an alarm during major disasters. It would soon be removed as a safety hazard, but it may have rung one last time in 1930.

The song is in a style scholars would call, with no ill intent, blues. She continues to tell the story, sometimes almost breathlessly:

> *I want you to listen, listen how the bell was ringing*
> *And how the people fell to the ground.*
> *They jumped through the windows, ran down the stairways and out the door.*
> *They was looking for safety, or they could not live no more.*
> *Oh, it was sad, sad, oh how sad*
> *When the Arcade Building burnt down.*
>
> *The brave firemen, they could not go home to eat.*
> *The Salvation women with coffees and cakes kept them up on their feet.*
> *But the Lord saved Clyde Davis, death was so nigh.*
> *Carl Melcher and his wife were separated by the fire.*
> *Oh, listen, listen, how the bell did ring*

All of her lyrics are journalistic in their accuracy, straight from the dailies. Then she breaks out of the music in an ad lib a little too shy to pass for scat, as the pianist plays. "Play it! Oh, it was sad that morning! Several people lost their lives when the Arcade Building burnt down. What a moan in Knoxville!"

In her lyrics, Leola Manning was kind to Carl Melcher, giving him the benefit of the doubt. But within a day of his death, Melcher had become a suspect, presumed by many to be the arsonist who had started the fire, an insurance scammer or a terrorist of some sort. Speculation wasn't about his guilt but about his methods and motives. Word was that he had set the fire with gasoline, igniting it with some kind of electric wire. One story claimed that it had gotten out of hand somehow and that he had hobbled down the alley in the direction of his apartment. For reasons of his own, perhaps to hide, he had climbed the outside stairs of a building, where he died. The call to the cab was interpreted as a flubbed getaway.

An autopsy showed that he had died of shock, not electrocution. There were more odd details. The barrel of Gulf gasoline that he had bought was found in the rubble, unscathed.

Clyde Davis, mentioned in Leola Manning's song—the man who had leapt from a window onto a pedestrian—was certain that the man who broke his fall was Carl Melcher. Later, another witness claimed that Melcher was on the scene helping the firefighters move hoses.

After a few days, an inquest exonerated Melcher. He was reportedly buried at Lynnhurst, in Fountain City, though there's no stone with his name on it in that well-known cemetery. Helen Melcher disappears from city directories after her husband's death.

Soon after, Leola Manning disappears, too—by that name, anyway. The Brunswick/Vocalion sessions were apparently a disappointment to all participants. The record company offered very little in the way of publicity or distribution, and music archivists believe that fewer than five hundred of the Manning 78s were ever printed. They're considered rare today. Some, surprisingly including Uncle Dave Macon's sessions, were never even released.

Manning apparently separated from her husband, evangelist William Manning, by 1931. In 1933, she was living on Doll Avenue, near old Five Points in East Knoxville. The name Leola Manning never appeared in Knoxville lists after that.

Over the years, some music scholars assumed that maybe she left the South, as did many black musicians, including Howard Armstrong and his band mates, to try their fortunes up North, in Chicago or New York.

Most of the St. James recordings were forgotten, even in Knoxville. In 1982, coinciding with the Knoxville Worlds Fair, a vinyl record album, *Historical Ballads of the Tennessee Valley*, came out. It included Leola Manning's "The Arcade Building Moan."

Then, early in the CD era, recordings of rarely heard American blues songs began appearing on European compilations. One, called *Rare Country Blues*, came out from Document Records in Vienna, Austria, in 1993. That project claimed to compile the "complete recorded works" of six underappreciated black musicians. On that CD are all six of Leola Manning's St. James recordings. The liner notes on the Austrian disk report that "Manning, who sounded something like Memphis Minnie, was another off-centre artist who recorded religious songs in a blues setting." The notes speculate that the accompanist heard on the recording is Chicago pianist Charles Avery, a regular on some Brunswick records. Other sources, including Joslyn Layne of the All Music Guide, claim that Manning accompanied herself—though her ad-libbed shout of "Play it!" on "The Arcade Building Moan" and "Play it, boys!" on "Satan Is Busy in Knoxville" would seem to suggest otherwise.

That 1993 CD caught the attention of some high-profile musicians, among them iconoclastic country rocker Steve Earle. When he came to town for a 1998 show, he baffled longtime Knoxvillians with questions about where the Arcade Building was. Jazz pianist Donald Brown is also a fan of the Leola Manning recordings.

In the 1990s, local jazz and blues singer Nancy Brennan Strange was entranced with a tape of Manning's songs and the woman's unusual voice, "cooler, lighter than the others" of her era. By 2000, she was asking around town whether anyone had ever heard of Leola Manning. No one had. But then she got to speak with elderly musician Howard Armstrong during one of his late-life concert visits to Knoxville. Armstrong, who had made recordings at the St. James, too, remembered a young, especially religious woman named Leola, who was a singer. He didn't know what happened to her—except that she had married a guitarist named Gene Ballinger.

Strange started over, revising her question: "Did you ever hear of a blues singer named Leola Ballinger?" She had better luck, except that the implication that the woman sang blues offended the first elderly lady she found who recognized the name. Within the Knoxville black community of the 1920s and '30s, the word "blues" implied something unholy, even pornographic.

Strange learned that Leola Manning Ballinger hadn't left town after all. The impromptu researcher found the answer at a cinderblock chapel called the True House of God on a hillside in East Knoxville where the sunsets can catch you off guard. A sign hung out front, reading, "Bishop B.J. Moore, Pastor."

The bishop, a singer herself, was named Bobbie Jean Moore. She was Leola Manning's daughter. She offered a sketch of the elusive singer's life. Her maiden name was Leola Ramey, and she was born in Chattanooga to an evangelist known to her followers as Mama Ramey. They moved to Knoxville about 1910, when Leola was still a little girl. She grew up evangelizing in tent shows in East Knoxville with her mother. Musician Howard Armstrong sometimes volunteered to drive her mother to shows. Later, the Rameys were acquainted with the Swan Silvertones, the famous black gospel singing group.

Bishop Moore recalled her mother telling her about a grisly murder near the Mountain View School, apparently the one she sang about in "Satan Is Busy in Knoxville." She had been troubled by the state of the city at the time she made the recordings at the St. James. "She believed God was angry with the people because so much was going on," Bishop Moore said. Moore seemed to settle years of speculation about the identity of the pianist: he was just a local friend named Gace Haynes, who lived in Lonsdale.

Eugene Ballinger, whom she married soon after her divorce, was a guitarist she and her mother had met on one of their evangelizing trips in Middlesboro, Kentucky. She raised eight kids in all and spent the rest of her time evangelizing in the streets, in Knoxville and other cities and towns in the region. She told her children about cutting six sides at the St. James with a famous jazz producer. Known as Elder

Ballinger in her later years, she thought of herself as a leader of a congregation, though she rarely had a brick-and-mortar church to call her own. She continued singing but always within the context of evangelism: "street work," as she called it.

Nancy Strange gave Bishop Moore a copy of the Austrian release. The recording artist's daughter was unaware of it. In fact, her mother, Leola Manning Ballinger, lived until 1995 but never knew that her music had been rereleased either on vinyl or in CD format.

Developers had hardly let the embers cool on the Arcade Building site before beginning on a new, much larger building, today known as the Grand Union and occupied by bank offices.

The solid old St. James Hotel was torn down without much fanfare in the early 1970s to make way for the Tennessee Valley Authority's massive headquarters campus. It was said to have been quite a tough demolition job.

The six songs that constitute the complete works of Leola Manning, later to be known as Elder Ballinger, are available on the Internet. Songs from her St. James sessions have appeared on several compilations. *Down In Black Bottom: Barrelhouse Mamas* features "Satan Is Busy in Knoxville." *Favorite Country Blues: Piano-Guitar Duets, 1929–35* includes, somewhat ironically, Leola Manning's thesis statement, "The Blues Is All Wrong."

The recordings Leola Manning made at the St. James have been listened to much more in the years since her death than they were in the sixty-five years before then.

# ERNIE AND BILL

L ong before dawn on that cold morning in early 1937, the old man we knew as Uncle Bill left his rented room near Knoxville College and made his way to Weaver's Grill on Union Avenue. He was the pastry chef at Weaver's, and it took an early start to have fresh-baked pies ready for the lunch crowd.

It was the unpretentious sort of place where customers would come in with a newspaper and read at the counter while they ate—mixed reports about the economy, troubling rumors from Europe. In the *News-Sentinel* that day was the latest report from popular reporter Ernie Pyle, whose syndicated column was kind of a travelogue of Depression-era America. His latest dispatch was from Oklahoma.

Few would have looked up when a stranger entered and passed toward the back. The white man in the trench coat was here on business. His thinning hair was already going gray. He looked older than thirty-six.

He went into the back room of the restaurant with a pad of paper and spent a long time chatting with Uncle Bill, who was finally taking a break. The man in the trench coat, the roving columnist known to his millions of readers by name but not by face, was Ernie Pyle. His travel dispatches always displayed wry wit and sympathy for regular folks.

He was from Indiana but lately seemed especially interested in this part of the country. He had been here about a year earlier, to write about the construction of Norris Dam. The day before, he had gone up to see his "old friend" again. He remarked on how lonely and dull a dam looks when it's finished.

In five or six years, he would be America's most famous war correspondent, so close to the front lines that he was always photographed wearing a helmet. But in 1937, there was no war. In Knoxville, Ernie Pyle wore a fedora.

Uncle Bill, the pastry chef Ernie Pyle found so interesting, was born a very long time ago, before the Civil War, with the name William Andrew Johnson. He had been a slave of Andrew Johnson, named by Johnson himself, for himself. The fact that he'd been a slave of Abraham Lincoln's vice president probably struck no one raised in East Tennessee as ironic. It was a complicated time, and many East Tennessee Unionists were slaveholders. His status as a slave wasn't affected by Lincoln's Emancipation Proclamation, which applied only to the rebellious portions of the Confederate states and excepted the entire state of Tennessee, as well as the slave states that didn't secede. Slavery was not thoroughly abolished throughout the states until the Thirteenth Amendment passed, about eight months after Johnson became president.

However, according to tradition, Johnson freed his own slaves a few months after Lincoln's proclamation, on August 8, 1863. By the time the Johnsons moved to Washington in early 1865 for Andrew's tragically short tenure as vice president, his household slaves were probably already legally free. William Johnson was probably not literally a president's slave but a president's servant who had recently been a slave.

Uncle Bill had served the Johnson family after abolition when they moved back home to Greeneville, and he stayed with them after President Johnson's death in 1875, and into the 1880s, when he moved to Knoxville. He was close to seventy, in the 1920s, when he became a publicity gimmick for a new attraction on Gay Street. The ex-slave of Andrew Johnson was hired as a doorman for the new Andrew Johnson Hotel. William eventually tired of standing up all day and gave it up for a more interesting job baking. It was a skill he had learned as a slave.

"When I was little," William Johnson told Pyle,

> *Mr. Andrew used to hold me on one knee and my sister on the other, and he'd rub our heads and laugh…One day, Mrs. Johnson called us all in and said we were free now. She said we were free to go, or we could stay if we wanted to.*

Ernie Pyle scribbled it all down and wrote up the rare interview for the next Thursday's column. "William Andrew Johnson is a happy old man with a distinction," he wrote. "He is, so far as he knows, the only living ex-slave of a president." Pyle's column appeared without comment in the *News-Sentinel* and dozens of other papers nationwide.

*William came to Knoxville many years ago. He never married, and he has no relatives at all now.*

*William had a keen disappointment last spring. President Roosevelt came to Knoxville to dedicate Norris Dam. William got it into his head that he wanted to shake hands with the president and tell him he was once a slave of a president. William thought President Roosevelt might be agreeable to shaking hands with him.*

*So he went to some of his white friends—some big men in the Chamber of Commerce—and asked them if they would fix it up. They told William they would try, but they didn't think anything could be done. Later they reported back that such a thing was impossible. William was upset about it.*

*Of course it wasn't impossible at all. William should have known better than to ask a Chamber of Commerce man. He should have asked a newspaper man.*

Maybe he had a point. The story about Ernie Pyle's lunch with William Johnson caught the eye of one influential reader: Franklin Roosevelt himself, who immediately sent Secret Service agents to Knoxville to pay Uncle Bill's way for an official White House visit. When the train arrived in Washington, reporters swarmed to get a picture of the pastry chef from Weaver's Grill. However, obliging Secret Service agents had fitted Uncle Bill with a porter's outfit to allow him to slip through the mobs unrecognized.

Johnson had an unexpectedly lengthy audience with President Roosevelt. According to one newspaper report, he commented that Andrew Johnson's White House "wasn't nothing as compared to the White House doin's today."

Pyle didn't record Johnson's words in phonetic dialect, but other reporters did—though they allowed that his accent was "unlike the typical Southern Negro dialect."

Roosevelt presented Johnson with a silver-headed cane inscribed with FDR's name. "Mr. Roosevelt's jist my kind of white folks," he was quoted as saying. "He reminds me a heap of Marse Johnson. I'd hate to see him in sich trouble as Marse Johnson got into."

Pyle followed up in a later column, telling his readers that this was "the happiest I've ever inadvertently made anybody." William Johnson was a sudden celebrity, interviewed on nationwide radio.

His fame didn't last long, even at home. Four years later, as the war started, Johnson was in a home for the indigent, no longer able to walk or support himself with a job. Popular local columnist Bert Vincent wrote a column pleading that someone donate a wheelchair for Uncle Bill.

William Andrew Johnson died in 1943, thought to be eighty-seven. Ernie Pyle, the young man who interviewed Uncle Bill at Weaver's, died less than two years later, shot by a Japanese sniper at Ie Shima.

# THE MAN IN THE BACKSEAT

Hank Williams is an American legend. Everybody knows that he was one of the largest figures in the history of country music, but country music wasn't big enough to contain him. He may not have lived to hear the phrase "rock 'n' roll," but some of his stuff sounds like it. Some of his music was blues, or gospel, with even an old minstrel show song thrown in here or there. While he was still alive, jazz artists and pop crooners were interpreting his music. The last hit he ever knew about had zydeco flavorings. Bob Dylan called him his favorite songwriter. Leonard Cohen wrote a song about him. Norah Jones, born a quarter century after his death, covered his song "Cold, Cold Heart" on her hit CD.

Hank changed the pop-music paradigm. Before Hank Williams, professional singers on the radio were about as likely to write their own songs as they were to tailor their own double-breasted suits. Songwriters were guys with ties and thick glasses who worked in cramped offices in Manhattan. Most popular singers didn't even play instruments. No one before Hank Williams had been as popular as a guitarist/singer/songwriter, a combination that became the standard for several varieties of American popular music.

If he had not died at age twenty-nine but had merely retired to Palm Springs and lived to the age of eighty-nine, Hank would still be considered a major figure in the development of American pop culture. He would still have his plaque in the Country Music Hall of Fame in Nashville. But his early death gave him a weird boost. To die young and, moreover, to die mysteriously lends an aura of religion never accorded to influential figures allowed their threescore and ten. Fate allows Hank Williams to remain forever young, an icon to each new generation born long after he was buried. He still has authority with musicians unrivaled by his contemporaries—the ones who didn't die young, the ones who got chubby and wore hairpieces and worked the Pigeon Forge / Branson circuit and did a lot of chuckling on cable talk shows.

Hank Williams's death, or his ghost, is the subject of too many country songs to enumerate here. Someone once did try to count them all and had to stop in the seven hundreds. It has been the subject of movies, Broadway musicals and bus tours, as well as several biographies, both personal and scholarly. Hardly any two tellings agree on all the details. But they all have to contend with several hours he spent in downtown Knoxville.

Hiram Williams grew up poor in rural Alabama between the world wars. Inspired by street singers, cowboy movies and radio stars like Roy Acuff, Hank picked up guitar and also fiddle and started singing. At fourteen, he was winning talent contests and forming a band called the Drifting Cowboys. About the same time, as if it all went together, he started drinking. Almost skeletally skinny—he was six-two when he wasn't slouching and 140 pounds—he washed out in his selective-service examination during World War II. He wrote songs and made recordings, and his early ones show a maybe unsustainable range of enthusiasms, from "Honky Tonkin'" and "Move It on Over" to "I Saw the Light."

After several false starts, including rejection from the Grand Ole Opry, his "Lovesick Blues" became a national hit in 1949, as did "I'm so Lonesome I Could Cry." The contrite Opry promptly revised its opinion of him, and for the next three years he was one of the most prolific and popular singers in the nation. By 1950, when he released "Why Don't You Love Me," his shows in arenas around the country were drawing crowds of over ten thousand. An even younger pop star, Tony Bennett, made a hit of Hank's song "Cold, Cold Heart." But his nearly constant back pain exacerbated his drug abuse, which was, by some accounts, pathological. In 1951, he was diagnosed with spina bifida occulta. An operation to improve it wasn't wholly successful.

The year 1952 was his worst. Though he may have been the country's biggest pop star, his life was out of control. His manager would routinely send the star on the road with two bodyguards to keep him from getting too drunk to perform. In May, Williams's wife, Audrey, divorced him; they had two children, including three-year-old Hank Jr. The settlement cut into his famously large salary. To hear him tell it, by the end of the year he had nothing but his last paycheck. In August, the Opry, weary of his no-shows, fired him. In September, he recorded "Kaw-Liga," "Take These Chains from My Heart" and "Your Cheatin' Heart." None was released until after his death.

In October, he secretly married a beautiful young divorcée named Billie Jean Jones, but he spent much of the next several weeks in and out of sanitariums, eventually diagnosed with acute alcoholism. The last sanitarium discharged him on December 13. At the time, his Cajun anthem "Jambalaya" was a national radio hit. Another single he released that fall was "I'll Never Get Out of this World Alive."

Hank Williams spent Christmas with his family in Montgomery, squiring Billie Jean around town in hopes that folks would see that she wasn't just a gold digger. He assured everyone that she was going to help him settle down. He had lined up holiday gigs in Charleston, West Virginia, and Canton, Ohio—his first big shows outside the South in several months. After his recent struggles with rehabilitation, he hoped that this would be the beginning of the rest of his career. He got some of his old Nashville pals, like steel guitarist Don Helms, to help him out. Several agreed to meet him for the Canton show. Homer and Jethro, the talented comedian-musician duo from Knoxville who were then enjoying some national fame, would be the openers.

On December 28, Williams put on a coat and tie and played his last show, a party for the Montgomery chapter of the American Federation of Musicians. It was mostly a union of jazz performers, not necessarily country fans, but he wowed them. They listened "attentively," according to one, "as if attending a concert by Benny Goodman."

Some friends thought he was in pretty good shape for a guy recovering from years of drug and alcohol abuse. Reporters described him as "tired looking," though, and other friends worried that he was seriously ill, having difficulty controlling his bladder. He had a bad night on December 29; he kept waking up. His wife asked, "Hank, what is the matter with you?" He answered, "Billie, I think I see God coming down the road."

The trip from Montgomery north seemed jinxed from the start. They originally intended to fly to Charleston, but the morning after Hank's bad night, there was snow on the ground. Driving seemed safer.

Williams enlisted eighteen-year-old Charles Carr, an Auburn freshman and sometime cabdriver, to drive his baby-blue 1952 Cadillac to Ohio. That model was a streamlined, sportier-looking car than later Cadillacs would be. Before he left, he reportedly got a shot of morphine from a Montgomery doctor.

They spent the night of the thirtieth in a Birmingham hotel. Carr, who had a reputation for reckless driving, got in trouble with a local cop for an illegal U-turn. They proceeded north. "Jambalaya" was on the car radio, and Williams asked Carr how he liked it. Carr answered, with teenage candor, that it didn't make any sense to him.

"That's 'cause you don't understand French," Williams retorted.

One story has them stopping in Fort Payne, Alabama, for breakfast, and another has them stopping for a meal in Chattanooga, where Williams left the waitress a fifty-dollar tip. They arrived in Knoxville late in the morning on New Year's Eve. Worried about getting to Charleston in time for the show, they decided to ditch the car in Knoxville and catch a plane north. A flight was scheduled to leave McGhee Tyson Airport at 3:30 p.m. The layover was long enough to consider a local radio appearance.

Knoxville was regionally famous in 1952 for its live-radio shows on two rival stations, WNOX and WROL, both with studios downtown on Gay Street. About fifteen years earlier, Williams's idol, Roy Acuff, had been playing on both stations. Either would likely have welcomed a drop-in appearance from Hank Williams. According to local grocer/politician/impresario Cas Walker, the chief advertiser and popular host of WROL's shows, Carr called and Walker invited him to bring Williams in for an unannounced appearance on *WROL Hayloft*. One biography mistakenly associates Walker's show with his rival WNOX's *Mid-Day Merry-Go-Round*. Details of previous Williams appearances in Knoxville are hard to come by, but Walker told the *Knoxville News-Sentinel* in early 1953 that Williams "had made a few singing appearances as a guest entertainer" on his WROL show. They seem to have respected each other.

However, Walker later said, "He never showed up, and it was probably because he was not feeling well." At the airport that afternoon, Williams boarded the 3:30 p.m. flight north. About two hours later, the pilot, discouraged by snow, returned to McGhee Tyson. Williams gave up on the New Year's Eve Charleston show and had Carr drive him into town.

Knoxville was an awkward city in 1952, still waiting for television to arrive, a year after Major Neyland's Vols won the national championship. The city was getting national criticism from watchdog groups for its "open toleration of vice," especially prostitution, but at the same time, the morally tortured city was still maintaining its ban on wine or liquor, by the drink or by the bottle. Bootlegging was rampant, though, and it was often a violent city, especially during the holidays. Christmas shootings in three separate households had left a mom, a dad and a teenager dead, not counting a husband-wife murder-suicide in Morristown. Still, many were convinced that Knoxville's greatest threat was not domestic violence but Communism. Praising red-baiting Senator Joe McCarthy, the *Knoxville Journal* stirred up suspicion about "Pinkos" and old resentments about the New Deal, which right-wingers still hoped President-elect Eisenhower would overturn. That one day, more than seven years after Roosevelt's death, the *Journal* ran two anti-FDR columns.

Iconic country music singer and songwriter Hank Williams rarely performed in Knoxville during his career but spent some of his final hours in the Andrew Johnson Hotel on Gay Street. *Courtesy of the Library of Congress.*

With champagne illegal, the holiday of New Year's Eve was low key by the standards of later eras. The Tennessee Theater and some other movie houses were hosting midnight shows. The city did host a dry "Gala New Year's Eve Show & Dance" at Chilhowee Park, featuring Wacky Red Murphy and local comedian/politician Archie Campbell in his trademark guise as "Grandpappy"—plus the

Cherokee Indian Square Dancers. (The following day's Chilhowee Park show makes the dawning of 1953 sound like a cultural watershed: the headliner was Louisiana R&B performer Lloyd Price, "that Lawdy Miss Claudy man," remembered as one of the founders of rock 'n' roll.)

As usual, most Knoxvillians were focused on their Vols, who were in Dallas for the New Year's Cotton Bowl game against the Texas Longhorns. Hundreds of Knoxville fans, including the ailing Major Neyland, were in Texas for the game. NBC would be broadcasting the game on national television, but not in Knoxville. The nearest NBC-TV affiliate was in Atlanta.

It was dark by 6:08 p.m., when Charles Carr and Hank Williams checked into the Andrew Johnson Hotel. The seventeen-story Andrew Johnson was the tallest building in East Tennessee. Almost twenty-five years old, its marble floors and ornate balustrades and ballroom spoke of an earlier, swankier era. It was still considered Knoxville's finest hotel. Its 350 rooms all had private bathrooms. The AJ catered to Smokies tourists in those days before there were many hotel rooms closer to the mountains, but in 1952, many Knoxvillians who could afford it came to the hotel restaurant to have a steak in elegant surroundings, accompanied by an organist playing popular songs and stylish classics.

Though its ballroom was sometimes a place to hear big horn–based jazz bands, whether the proprietors liked it or not the hotel had also developed a genuine country music heritage. In the mid-1930s, the top floor had been home to WNOX studios. Its rambunctious live shows didn't mesh with the hotel's posh image, and when the elevators were loaded with country music fans going all the way to the top, there were complaints. The station was eventually asked to move its shows elsewhere.

Before it did, however, one of the most promising stars who played there was a redheaded Knoxvillian named Roy Acuff. By the time he made it to the Opry, Acuff had become the idol of a thousand poor white kids in Alabama, including the young Hank Williams. Williams would imitate, and improve on, Acuff's high-lonesome croon. (Acuff later knew Williams but, uncomfortable with the younger performer's drug abuse, was said not to be a great admirer.)

The Andrew Johnson also had some connections to the fates of interesting celebrities. Aviator Amelia Earhart had stayed there in 1936, the year before her disappearance. While in the hotel, she told a newspaper reporter that flying was a dangerous business, and she didn't really expect to see old age. In 1943, the great Russian composer and pianist Sergei Rachmaninoff stayed there after performing at UT's Alumni Hall. Meant to be just one stop on his American tour, it turned out to be the final performance of his long career. In pain from an undiagnosed cancer, he canceled the rest of his tour and died about three months later.

Built in 1928, the Andrew Johnson Hotel already had associations with the beginning of the career of Roy Acuff—and the end of the career of Russian composer Sergei Rachmaninoff—before Hank Williams checked in on New Year's Eve 1952. *Circa 1945 postcard image courtesy of Mark Heinz.*

The desk clerk on duty on the evening of December 31 was Dan McCrary. He thought that the teenage chauffeur who approached the counter looked nervous. He didn't see Williams but was aware that Carr's boss needed porters to help him to his room. Carr told McCrary that they intended to stay the night.

According to some secondhand accounts, Hank Williams had stayed there before. Years later, porters would boast that he had holed up at the AJ for days at a time, tipping them as they kept him supplied with booze, drugs and girls. There are, inevitably, stories that he purchased moonshine from a Knoxville supplier that night. Other stories published in biographies have him appearing at St. Mary's Hospital, where he allegedly got a booster of morphine from his unnamed "usual" doctor.

What's known for certain is that Carr ordered a couple of steak dinners from the dining room. The teenager ate the steak; Williams picked at his but didn't finish it. According to reports released in the days to come, Williams began hiccupping and went into convulsions.

Sometime during the night, Dr. Paul H. Cardwell arrived. A clean-cut physician in his fifties, Cardwell kept a modest office about three blocks away from the hotel, on Cumberland Avenue, in a building called the George Apartments, where he also lived. He had developed a relationship with the hotel as a sort of informal house physician. How and why he was called, and whether Williams's Alabama physician/supplier had anything to do with it, is one of the many questions of that night. Whether Dr. Cardwell knew who Hank Williams was is unclear. He might have been the only handy doctor downtown on New Year's Eve.

Cardwell later described Williams as "very drunk" and said that there were some pills visible in the room. He gave Williams two injections, one of vitamin B-12 and one of morphine. He told investigators in the days afterward that the morphine was called for to control Williams's convulsions. If there is any truth to the St. Mary's story, it wasn't the only dose of morphine he got in Knoxville that day.

After Dr. Cardwell's injections, Williams lay down on his hotel bed, fell asleep and later rolled off the bed and onto the floor.

Either Williams or Carr changed their plans and decided not to spend the whole night at the Andrew Johnson. Considering how the ill-fated trip was going, it might have made sense to get an early start to make the Ohio show, still scheduled for the night of January 1 and more than four hundred miles away. Carr checked out of the Andrew Johnson at 10:45 p.m. According to some accounts from witnesses at the hotel, and eventually the official police report, Hank Williams was not conscious at the time. The only sounds of life were two "coughing sounds" he made while he was carried out. For decades to come, doctors, detectives and biographers would speculate about whether those two sounds could have been made by a dead man.

However, in recent years, an elderly porter who says he was there that night has claimed that Williams was not only conscious as he left but also making jokes about his drinking, and he left the hotel on his own two feet. The contradictions of that evening would continue to accumulate.

Porters unnamed in the available sources loaded Hank Williams into the back of the blue Cadillac. The shortest route to Ohio would have taken him north on Gay Street, which was quiet at that hour except for some boys milling around on the sidewalks with firecrackers in their pockets, waiting for midnight. He would have driven by the Tennessee Theater, which was then opening its doors for an 11:15 p.m. showing of a Broderick Crawford comedy called *Stop, You're Killing Me.*

In those days before the interstates, Carr would likely have driven out of town via Magnolia Avenue. That New Year's Eve, Ken Jarnigan worked at Troutman's 24-Hour Esso on Magnolia at Winona. He was used to seeing celebrities at his station, especially pro wrestlers on their way to Chilhowee Park. Even country star Ferlin Husky stopped in once.

Sometime before 11:00 p.m. that night, a Cadillac pulled in. As Jarnigan pumped the gas, the man in the backseat concerned him. "He was dressed up in dress clothes, white shirt, no tie," he recalled years later. "He was foaming at the mouth. I told that young man, 'He looks like he's dead.' The guy said, 'Don't worry about him. He's drunk and passed out.'"

Their route would have taken them right past Archie Campbell's country/ comedy show at Chilhowee Park. Soon after that, they would get on U.S. Highway 11W. Though it seems a roundabout way to go north today, 11W, known as Rutledge Pike in Knox County, was probably the best route to eastern Ohio in the early 1950s. But the curvy, narrow road was already known for accidents, developing a reputation as "Bloody 11W."

Most standard accounts imply that Carr didn't stop again in Knox County. However, one lady who spoke to this reporter claimed that her late husband, who ran a drive-in short-order and beer store on 11W in the Three Points area of the northeast corner of Knox County, told her that the Cadillac had stopped there. The proprietor, a former zinc miner, usually closed by 10:00 p.m. or so but happened to be open unusually late that night, maybe for the holiday. She said, as her husband used to tell it, there was not just one car but two that pulled up. He assumed that they were musicians, except for one hitchhiker, a "serviceman." He said that at least two men got out and had something to eat. One man stayed in the car. When the proprietor learned that the man in the backseat was Hank Williams, he went out in hopes of meeting him. But Williams was asleep, and the other men told the proprietor that the singer was drunk.

There are other stories of the blue Cadillac stopping here or there on its way out of town. If they're all true, Carr and Williams had a very busy night before they left Knox County. Perhaps none of them are invented, but it's likely that all of them are warped by the passage of time.

By 11:45 p.m., Carr had left Knox County, driving north on 11W near Blaine. Passing a car, he pulled into the oncoming lane and narrowly missed a southbound vehicle. Unfortunately for Carr, the driver was a state trooper. Corporal Swann Kitts turned around and pulled over the Cadillac. "I noticed Williams and asked Carr if he could be dead, as he was pale and blue-looking," Kitts later recalled. "But he said Williams had drunk six bottles of beer and a doctor had given him two injections to help him sleep."

Kitts had Carr follow him to Rutledge. As Williams remained in the backseat, Carr met the justice of the peace and paid the twenty-five-dollar fine. One of several mysteries of the trip is the presence, noted by Patrolman Kitts, of an unnamed soldier traveling with Carr at the Rutledge stop.

Then Carr drove more than two hundred miles northeast, through the night. He passed through Bristol, the site of the major recordings of the Carter Family and Jimmy Rodgers twenty-five years earlier, which had helped popularize early country music. The yodeling Rodgers, in particular, had been an inspiration to Hank Williams. At a local taxi company, Carr picked up a second driver, Donald Surface.

Before his own death, Surface claimed that Williams had been alive in Bristol, awake and walking around the car. Carr's account differed; he said he had talked to Williams there but not that he was walking around. Surface got off somewhere in West Virginia. Even the detail of where is controversial.

As the dawn of New Year's Day approached, Carr, with or without Surface, began to notice the silence in the backseat. Arriving in Oak Hill, West Virginia, a small town of thirty-five hundred southeast of Charleston, at about 5:30 a.m., he finally pulled over at either a drive-in movie theater or a Pure Oil station (a discrepancy between the original police report and Carr's later memories). He found that his boss was cold to the touch, unresponsive and, in fact, already stiff. When he pushed Williams's hand, it sprang back. Carr sped to the local hospital, six miles away, where Hank Williams was pronounced dead on arrival. Apparently, all of the doctors on duty to examine a body on a holiday morning were foreign-born. An Italian intern named Nunnari estimated, at 7:00 a.m., that Williams might have been dead for six hours. The state lab in Charleston found alcohol in his blood but apparently did not test for other drugs. A Russian physician who spoke little English performed the autopsy. He described the cause of death as an "insufficiency" in the heart's right ventricle. He also added one more twist to the night's tangle of mysteries. He observed that, sometime not too long ago, somebody had beaten Williams.

Still another puzzle was the scrawled note found in the backseat of the Cadillac. An apparent fragment of a song about separation from a lover, sometimes assumed to have been Williams's last work: "We met we lived and dear we loved / Then came that fatal day." Undated, it could well have been written earlier in the trip or even back in Alabama.

The news of Hank Williams's death traveled fast and even made it into some holiday editions of newspapers. Hank Williams died in Oak Hill, West Virginia. Newspapers reported that he was thirty-seven years old. Many thought that he looked a decade or two older than that. In fact, he was only twenty-nine.

When word reached the shocked crowd in Canton, the audience sang, "I Saw the Light." Williams's services in Montgomery drew the biggest crowd since Jefferson Davis's funeral there in 1889. In 1953, reporters found it remarkable that the crowd of mourners at Hank Williams's funeral was biracial.

By January 2, as sports pages reported the glum news of the Vols' loss to Texas in the Cotton Bowl, headlines were pondering, "Mystery Shrouds Death of Singer Hank Williams. Hillbilly Star Believed Dead Hours Before Taken to the Hospital."

Swann Kitts, the officer who had pulled over the Cadillac Carr was driving in Blaine, was given authority to investigate. It was an unusual situation, considering that he was also a witness. "After investigating the matter," Kitts concluded,

*I think that Williams was dead when he was dressed and carried out of the hotel. Since he was drunk and was given the injections and could have taken some capsules earlier, with all this he couldn't have lasted over an hour and a half or two hours.*

In spite of Carr's insistence that Williams had spoken in Bristol and must have died in the Virginias, Kitts's report to the Tennessee Highway Patrol concluded that Williams had most likely died in the hotel and that porters had carried his corpse out to the car. Biographer Colin Escott, citing the medical records and the extent of Williams's rigor mortis upon arrival at the hospital, agrees that Williams probably died in Knoxville. That version seems to have been accepted by the family.

In the decades since, most of the witnesses have died or vanished. Charles Carr, who was quiet about the case for many years, survived into the 2000s and spoke to reporters late in life, maintaining his story that Williams was talking to him in the car more than one hundred miles beyond Knoxville. In 2009, a man who said he was a teenage porter at the Andrew Johnson in 1952 claimed that Williams was conscious as he left and even joked with the porters about the wages of sin.

Discrepancies in the various stories of the death of Hank Williams will likely persist forever, just like the discrepancies in the gospels.

# THE SECRET DIVA OF LOUISE AVENUE

Her gravestone in New Gray Cemetery on Western Avenue is so low and small that you don't notice it unless you look carefully. Even when she was alive, it is safe to say that most folks downtown around 1960 wouldn't have paid much attention to this old black lady with cat's-eye glasses, her short graying hair parted on the side. She lived with her daughter in East Knoxville and never stepped before an audience of people except on Sunday mornings at the Patton Street Church of God, about a block south of East Vine, where she was a member of the choir. Even there, she never stood out; she never even soloed.

She lived a modest life with her middle-aged daughter, Helen Goode, in their house on Louise Avenue at the corner of Parham Street. Goode had a respected position as principal of the old Simpson School, a black elementary school in Vestal. She and her mother were better off than many in their neighborhood near Five Points. They had an upright piano and a television that they looked at now and then. When the older lady went out, no one stared or asked her for her autograph. She had lived in Knoxville for more than a decade, but only a few Knoxvillians knew who she was.

Anonymity seems to have suited her then, though to her it may have seemed novel. Ida Cox was, simply, one of the most famous people who ever lived in Knoxville. Back in the 1920s, at the crest of the Jazz Age, she had been known on thousands of record labels in thousands of Victrolas coast to coast as "Ida Cox, the Uncrowned Queen of the Blues."

In her prime, she sang thousands of dates in nightclubs and tent shows across the nation and cut dozens and dozens of singles on 78s. Among them

Ida Cox (1896?–1967), the "Uncrowned Queen of the Blues," at the height of her fame, probably in the 1930s. The signature is to the Knoxville disc jockey Lynn Westergaard, who took an interest in her late-life career. *Courtesy of Tennessee Archive of Moving Image and Sound.*

was a song she wrote herself and recorded in 1924: "Wild Women Don't Have the Blues." Decades later, the song has taken on a career of its own, inspiring bumper stickers, T-shirt slogans and titles of bestselling novels. It appears on many modern CDs, in versions by singers as unlikely as Lyle Lovett.

# This Obscure Prismatic City

In 1938, she starred in the legendary John Hammond revue, *From Spirituals to Swing*, at Carnegie Hall, alongside Count Basie, Benny Goodman, Lionel Hampton, Charlie Christian, Fletcher Henderson and Big Bill Broonzy. Cox herself sang with a band that included pianist James P. Johnson and saxophone legend Lester Young. It became a classic recording on the Vanguard label, rereleased on CD in the twenty-first century.

Just a few years after that hubbub, she vanished. She dropped out of sight so thoroughly that many of her old friends assumed she must have died. When the album version of "From Spirituals to Swing" was printed in 1960, Hammond wrote the liner notes: "The whereabouts of Ida Cox, one of the very great blues singers of the '20s and '30s, is uncertain, and we can only hope that the rumors of her passing are false."

They were false indeed, and as it turned out, the old lady on Louise Avenue had one more important recording to make.

**\*\*\***

"Try to speak up as loud as you can, Miss Cox," says a young man's voice. Her conversation surprises you, coming through over modern equipment that she wouldn't have recognized. She sounds gracious and genteel, in the modest way of polite old southern ladies.

"I got millions of compliments," Ida Cox says of her early years. "But, you know, I didn't receive it. You see, I thought I was just hollering for no reason, and the man was paying me."

She's speaking in 1961, into the microphone of a reel-to-reel tape recorder brought into her house by a young white man. Tall, clean-shaven and wearing horn-rimmed glasses, Lynn Westergaard was a twenty-four-year-old announcer for local TV and radio stations. His last name was well known; his father was local radio legend R.B. "Dick" Westergaard, longtime manager of WNOX and the quiet force behind that station's influential country-music heyday.

The younger Westergaard, a piano player himself, knew and respected several of the country stars who played on his dad's station. But his personal passion was jazz. At twenty-four, he could talk about the old-time Jazz Age greats as easily as the current bebop pioneers. In early '61, he had heard some intriguing news from his friend Harry Nides. A versatile musician, Nides (pronounced Nidus) was both a Knoxville Symphony Orchestra violinist and a country fiddler. Nides, who kept up with the business, had heard that John Hammond—probably the century's most influential popular music impresario—had taken a break from promoting his latest find, a young

95

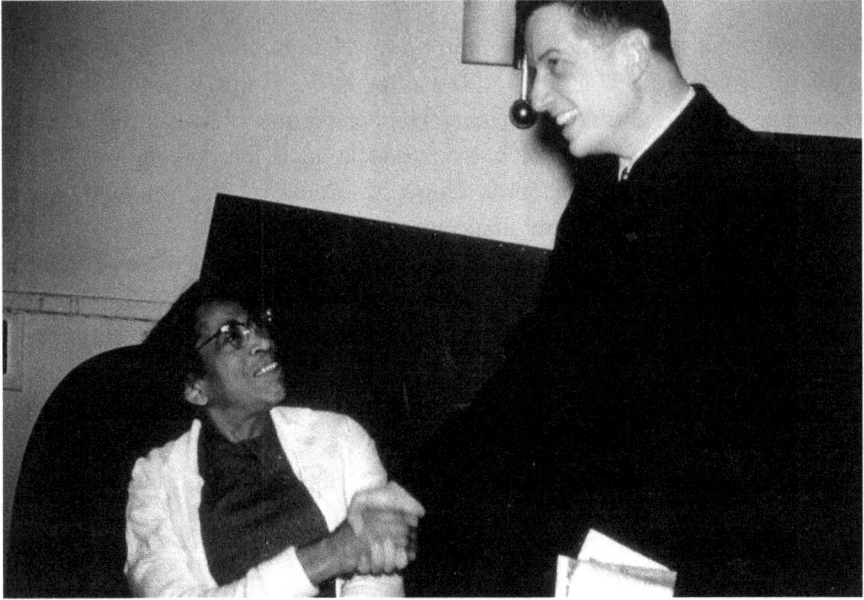

A photo of blues singer Ida Cox and legendary music promoter John Hammond at the time of her final recording in New York in 1961. The photo was taken by Knoxville disc jockey and pianist Lynn Westergaard. *Courtesy of Tennessee Archive of Moving Image and Sound.*

Jewish kid from Minnesota who went by the name Bob Dylan, to try to track down an old friend.

Many assumed that Ida Cox had died young, as had so many of her contemporaries—Bessie Smith, Ma Rainey, Mamie Smith. In 1960, Hammond ran an ad in *Variety* magazine seeking information about the whereabouts of the Uncrowned Queen of the Blues. He owed her some royalties from a recording she had made twenty years before, and he didn't want to believe the rumors that she was dead.

Nides heard about Hammond's search and told Westergaard that he'd heard Ida Cox was living quietly in East Knoxville. Westergaard looked up Ida Cox in the phone book—it was as simple as that—and gave her a call. He thinks it was in February 1961 when he found her house on Louise Avenue. He introduced himself and befriended a legend.

Westergaard's modest manner of talking about his old buff leather valise leads you to expect something much less astonishing inside it. There, you'll find an original vinyl copy of the LP *From Spirituals to Swing*, some recent CD compilations of Ida Cox's work in the '20s, plus another LP called *Blues for Rampart Street*. There are several black-and-white glossies of Cox in her prime, autographed to "Mr. Westergaard," as well as newer photos of her with musicians in a recording session.

Ida Cox and Lynn Westergaard, the local radio man who befriended her and remembered the experience many years later as a high point of his career. *Courtesy of Tennessee Archive of Moving Image and Sound.*

There's an essay from the *New Yorker* in 1961. There's Ida Cox's recording contract. And there's a cassette-tape copy of part of Westergaard's interview with the singer.

The tape sounds like it was made yesterday. He asks her when and where she was born. Even then, the published authorities about Ida Cox disagreed about that. She seems surprised by the question, as if she had never thought much about it. "Eighteen and sixty-eight?" she offers gamely, though obviously puzzled, perhaps as the result of a stroke some years before. Westergaard suggests 1896. Some sources say 1894 or even 1889. She agrees that 1896 is close enough. She's more certain of the fact that she was born in the tiny community of Toccoa, Georgia.

"We lived on a farm, but we had everything that anyone else could want: hogs, cows, chickens. No doubt about it, we lived real well." They moved from one small town to another, from Toccoa to Lawrenceville to Cedartown. Most of her singing in those days was in the Baptist church: old-time slow spirituals.

"I liked to sing, period," she says. "I liked to sing anything. I just liked to sing. I loved church songs, which I do today. I love to listen to a record of good church.

"Don't you?" she asks, in a way that doesn't allow for a less-than-enthusiastic response.

Sometime before World War I, a traveling show called the *Georgia Black & Tan Minstrels* came through town. The manager was Ed Grizzard, of Columbus,

Georgia, and he told her she sounded like a professional. "He couldn't believe I had just started singing." Maybe it was the flattery that pulled her.

"I ran away when I was sixteen years old, to go on stage," she told Westergaard. (She had told other interviewers she was just fourteen.)

> *I ran away with a minstrel show. There was a couple with the show that I got acquainted with, Charles and Lily White. They told me how I could get away, and they'd help me.*
>
> *So I told them what they would have to do was to come to my house one night after the show. I told them what night to come. I'd leave my clothes packed sitting outside the window—and for them to just take the bag with my clothes in it back to the car. And later on, I'd be on out. Oh, dear, that's how I got away.*

Westergaard asked her what her mother had thought about it. "Of course, she didn't want to hear about it," Cox responded. "Anyway, I had just gone." She said she never returned to her hometown except once, rolling through on a train.

She stayed with that show for a year and then joined another. She sang ragtime tunes, ballads mostly. "Ragtime songs was what we called them in those days. Later years, of course, they started calling them blues."

She mentioned a couple she remembered: "Put Your Arms Around Me, Honey, Hold Me Tight" and "Meet Me Tonight in Dreamland." Westergaard asked her if she sang these ballads with a blues feel, even at the beginning.

"I imagine I did," she answered. "I guess I did. It's all I knew."

Then she joined the faster lanes of vaudeville: "To my recollection, I played so many, I played every state in this union."

Approaching age twenty, she settled down for a while in Chicago, working at the Monogram Theater and the Grand. It was there that she became acquainted with Louis Armstrong, a young trumpeter who accompanied her in a speakeasy, and King Oliver. She knew all of the greats and even sang with Jelly Roll Morton on occasion.

"I met Ma Rainey when I was playing an old Airdome Theater," she recalled on Westergaard's tape.

> *She was much more popular than I. She had been in show business for quite some time. Ma Rainey was just like a mother, not to one but to all who knew her. She was a lovely person. I was even in her home in Columbus, Georgia. I was playing there, and I remember her coming down to the theater and sitting [in] I think the second or third row from the front. Her health had begun failing*

*her then. And she never lived to overcome this devil sickness.* [Ma Rainey was in her fifties when she died of heart disease in 1939.]

*Ethel Waters was a fine fellow, a wonderful person to know. We were very, very friendly. She always liked the style of hats I wore. She always paid me for them, gave me more than I paid for them. I guess I haven't seen Ethel in twenty years. I see her quite often on TV. I always admired her. She was a wonderful singer. And still is—what she'd sing, she does only church songs now.*

*Bessie Smith, Bessie too, Bessie was a wonderful girl and we were very friendly. Bessie, Clara, Ethel.*

She coughs, and that's the end of the tape. She had been talking about her old friends and hadn't yet gotten to her own career. Westergaard recorded much more but doesn't know what happened to the rest.

Ida spent thirty years in show business, witnessing what may have been the most fertile era in the history of American popular music. She grew up on spirituals and learned ragtime. When jazz and the blues arrived, she was right there.

Her music didn't make much of a distinction between the two. In 1923, at the very dawn of jazz recording, she cut her first commercial 78s. Most of her songs are blues in their basic lyric form. Her accompaniment in the early days was not a guitar but a small jazz band. The piano, clarinet and cornet, sometimes with a banjo or drums thrown in for percussion, had a wild sound like a particularly uninhibited klezmer band. Ida Cox was from the country, sure enough, but she didn't live there anymore.

In her personal life, it is fair to say that she paid her dues. She had a baby she named Helen, apparently before she was twenty. Somewhere in there, she married—first, a showman named Adler Cox and then her favorite pianist, Jesse Crump. There are stories that she married a third time.

In her 1924 song, "Confidential Blues," you get the feeling she knows what she's singing about:

> *Lord, I went to Europe, was about to be a good man's wife*
> *But along came somebody and told him all of my past life.*
> *Goodbye, people, please don't spread the news*
> *Because anything I've told you is strictly confidential blues.*

She didn't have the experience of Ma Rainey, and she wasn't nearly as beautiful as Bessie Smith. Ida Cox had something else altogether. A big part of it was the fact that she wrote many of her own songs, a habit very unusual for vocalists of her day.

Between 1923 and 1940, she cut at least sixty-five records. Many are mournful dirges from the point of view of a woman heartbroken because her man is gone, either because he left her or because she shot him, like "Graveyard Bound Blues":

> *When they carried him to the graveyard, Lord, how I did rave*
> *And when they lowered his coffin, I jumped right down in his grave.*

Paramount often billed her as the Uncrowned Queen of the Blues, but she went by other nicknames, as well. One of the most telling was a billing she got at the Apollo in 1934: "The Sepia Mae West." Like her contemporary, Ida Cox was buxom and proud of it, favoring low-cut dresses. And like Mae West, she sang frankly about sex, sometimes in a tough, bawdy, saloon-tempered style. But some of Ida's lyrics might have made Mae blush—"Handy Man," for example, one of the songs she sang for Westergaard's tape:

> *He greases my griddle, creams my wheat, churns my butter, chops my meat*
> *Oh, that man is such a handy man...*
> *You ought to see that brand-new stopper he uses in my machine.*

Even more risqué was a later song, her own "One-Hour Mama":

> *I'm a one-hour Mama*
> *So no one-minute Papa*
> *Ain't the kind of man for me...*
> *I don't want no lame excuses*
> *About my loving being so good*
> *That you couldn't wait no longer*
> *Now I hope I'm understood.*

Sometimes she would illustrate her lyrics with a "shimmy dance." Men would come to see her shows and enjoy them in the same way they might have enjoyed a striptease show. But they would also get a stern lesson about one woman's will. Several of her songs refer to "monkey men," whom Ida, or her persona, defined as men who were good only for sex—and not very good for that. In her early classic, "Chicago Monkey Man Blues," she sings:

> *I've got a monkey man here, and a monkey man over there.*
> *If monkey men were money, I'd be Chicago's millionaire...*

# This Obscure Prismatic City

*I've got fourteen men now and only want one more*
*And as soon as I get that one I'll let the fourteen go.*

"Bear-Mash Blues" (1924) is more mournful, but with a similar situation:

*I got two men, can't tell them apart.*
*Only one's my living, the other one's my heart.*
*The one's my living, he won't let me be.*
*But the one that's my heart don't care for me.*

Among her early sidemen were some of the greats of the day: Tommy Ladnier, trombonist; the great Johnny Dodds, New Orleans clarinet master; and even Fletcher Henderson, just before his greatest fame as the effective inventor of the big band sound, played piano on several Ida Cox releases in 1924. He was billed as one of her "Blue Spells."

That was the year she recorded the first version of what is now her most famous song and one of her best. She wrote it herself:

*I never was known to treat no one man right.*
*I keep 'em working hard both day and night...*
*You won't get nothing by being an angel child.*
*You better change your ways and get real wild.*
*Because wild women don't worry.*
*Wild women don't have the blues.*

She is known to have performed in Knoxville at least once during her prime, in 1930 at the Gem Theater on old Vine Street. (Torn down during urban renewal, the Gem was just east of what is now the intersection of Summit Hill and Central.) She likely performed here other times as well.

According to most sources, it was in 1945—the date was April 12, the same day that President Roosevelt died—that Ida Cox was performing at the Moonglow nightclub in Buffalo, New York, when she grew dizzy and then blacked out. She had suffered a serious stroke that left her face partially paralyzed.

She eventually moved to Knoxville to live with her daughter. Helen Goode was a Knoxville College graduate who had married a local man. She had been working here as a schoolteacher since the '30s. Ida herself had never lived here, but, as she said, "I knew Knoxville all right" from her appearances at the Gem and perhaps elsewhere.

Shaken by her illness, she reassessed her life and returned to the religion of her childhood. Over the next decade, she fell out of touch with all of her old showbiz acquaintances. She claimed that she never even thought about the life she left behind. "There wasn't anything I could do about it," she told one reporter.

Reenter John Hammond, the blues impresario. After he wrote his essay wondering about Ida Cox's fate, he ran the ad in *Variety*. Through a grapevine that included the manager of Knoxville's Gem Theater, word came to Cox and to an ambitious young radio reporter.

They made an unusual pair, especially in 1961, when many Knoxville restaurants, schools and movie theaters were still segregated: the clean-cut white man from West Knoxville and the black blues legend at least forty years his senior. The first desegregationist sit-ins in Knoxville had occurred less than a year before. Westergaard might have been mistaken for a civil rights volunteer.

"She was kind of like a grandmother," Westergaard recalls. "She had a sweet, soft side. But you could see under her grandmotherly demeanor that she had had a difficult life."

He admits that he saw opportunities for his own radio career in Ida's return to recording. But as a radio man, he saw that the job at hand was to get some demo tapes to New York. "My main purpose was to see if she could sing well enough to record," he recalls. Along the way, he came to think of himself as her de facto manager. (According to some written accounts, John Hammond himself came to Knoxville to visit Ida Cox and make some tapes; according to others, Chris Albertson of Riverside Records came to town to make the tapes. Westergaard never heard Cox mention any such visits.)

For Westergaard's tape, Ida needed an accompanist, of course. Westergaard himself played piano with her some, as did a woman friend of Ida's. Part of his tape had Cox singing a couple of old blues numbers and becoming frustrated with a piano player who wasn't playing like she was used to. "Looky, looky," she said. "You know the blues, don't you? The down-home blues, the good ole, everyday blues."

She finally settled on a more tested performer, a nightclub piano player well known around town, Charlie Boyd. He lived next door.

Westergaard recalls that Cox seemed insecure, as if she wasn't sure it was going to work. "She felt that she was out of the loop," he recalls, "after so many years out of the mainstream."

She had reason to be uncertain, and Westergaard knew it. She was about sixty-five—maybe a few years older than that—and, of course, she'd had a stroke from which she hadn't fully recovered. When she spoke, part of her face didn't move.

As Boyd played her upright, Ida Cox sang rowdy old blues songs into Westergaard's reel-to-reel. Westergaard witnessed a transformation come over the shy old lady. "She could stand up and belt it out like nobody's business," he says. He knew then that it was going to work.

He sent the tapes to Riverside to convince anyone who needed convincing that an Ida Cox recording would be feasible and worthwhile. He also needed to convince Ida Cox herself.

He recalls that she often seemed reluctant to record again, with concerns that apparently went beyond her vocal quality. She may have viewed her 1945 stroke as an act of God; as she had recovered, she had mended her ways and given up the blues altogether.

Learning that she would be traveling alone, Westergaard went along with her to help out. They flew to New York in April, to a studio on the fourth floor of Radio City Music Hall. It was a memorable day, by coincidence sixteen years to the day since Ida Cox had suffered the stroke that might have ended her career.

Of course, Jazz Age blues weren't trendy in April 1961. The two big songs on the radio that month were the Marcels' doo-wop version of "Blue Moon" and Del Shannon's "Runaway." Jazz itself had changed radically from the dance music it had been in the '20s and '30s into the deeper, more contemplative strains of bebop. Older folks remembered who Ida Cox was, though, and crowded into the studio to see her.

Westergaard was impressed by the hubbub. John Hammond himself was there; Rockettes came and went through the studio. It was an unusual session in that it had attracted several music critics, the sort who would ordinarily wait until the record came out before paying it any mind. Some in the studio described it as the best-attended recording session in memory.

Even the sidemen were stars. Trumpeter Roy Eldridge, sax man Coleman Hawkins and bassist Milt Hinton were her band, along with drummer Jo Jones, who had backed her up in that big Carnegie Hall show back in '38. "I heard her call them boys," Westergaard recalls. The men were all in their fifties, all jazz legends.

Westergaard says that Hawkins was late. Ida Cox's old pianist and former husband, Jesse Crump, had also been unable to make it, and that was a disappointment to Cox. Boogie-woogie stylist Sammy Price filled in on piano. Westergaard says he was in awe of being in the same studio with some of his jazz heroes. He took pictures of everything he saw.

When Coleman Hawkins arrived, having overslept, he and Eldridge sat in folding chairs and blew, and during breaks, they shared a bottle of Beefeaters gin. But they played so well that the album would become almost as well known for its instrumental breaks as for Ida's singing. They decided they wouldn't try to imitate the sound of thirty or forty years before but reinterpret the old music with modern jazz accompaniment.

Ida Cox wore a white sweater as she sang; she said it was chilly in the studio. On the recording, her voice sounded aged, sometimes a little off key, but it still had her trademark get-out-of-the-way muscle to it. She didn't put up with any monkey men's tricks in her youth, and she wasn't about to start at this stage of her life. She sang several songs, including "Graveyard Dream Blues," "Moanin' Groanin' Blues," "'Fore Day Creep" and her classic:

> *Wild women don't worry*
> *Wild women don't have the blues.*

In the album's title tune, she made a subtle change in the lyrics she had recorded in 1924:

> *I'm going down to some café*
> *I wanna hear that colored jazz band play.*

In 1961, during the civil rights era, some had objected to the word "colored"; this time, she substituted the word "Creole."

The session was over in six hours.

Ida Cox was a celebrity in New York that week. She appeared on Merv Griffin's quiz show called *Play Your Hunch*, in which blindfolded panelists were expected to guess who they were talking to as Ida Cox wailed "Put Your Arms Around Me, Honey, Hold Me Tight." They failed.

Whitney Bailliet of the *New Yorker* interviewed her at length in her room at the Paramount Hotel. "Guess who was in and out of town last week, and after a 20-year absence, at that!" read the *New Yorker*'s "Talk of the Town" column. "Ida Cox, the legendary blues singer." The long article described Cox as "tallish, straight-backed, gray-haired, and handsomely proportioned," looking "several decades younger than her age." Bailliet marveled that Cox had been "living in total obscurity in Knoxville, Tenn."

Riverside paid Cox $250 for her work. Westergaard complained that she had signed a contract for $500, plus 5 percent royalties. Today, he doesn't know whether she ever received the balance.

Westergaard himself was never cut into the deal. He says that his preoccupation with Ida Cox that spring cost him his job at WATE; he found a job with an Atlanta radio station and has lived there ever since. It also cost him on a more personal level. His first child, Mark, was born the day he was in the studio with Cox. Missing his son's birth seems to be his only regret about the experience.

Riverside released *Blues for Rampart Street* a few weeks later, and the album got rave reviews from *High Fidelity* and other music magazines. It might have seemed like a comeback.

Cox would have none of it. "I don't want to ever make a record again," she told a reporter. "I just did this one because the people wanted me to. I hope God doesn't think it was a sin. I've prayed for Him to forgive me if He thinks it was."

"I mean to do the best I can," she had told Bailliet, before the session. "But then I'm going back home. Whoom, like that."

Then Ida Cox was content to disappear again to her cloistered life on Louise Avenue. She made no more records. In Atlanta, Westergaard occasionally got a scrawled postcard from her, usually asking about the health of his family, especially the son who was born on the day she made her last recording. (Mark Westergaard is raising a family of his own in Montana, where he prospects for natural resources.)

Ida Cox lived to see the removal of her old church, Patton Street Church of God, through urban renewal, which claimed the Gem Theater, as well.

Suffering from cancer in 1967, Cox was admitted to Knoxville's Baptist Hospital. Westergaard visited her only days before she died. She had spent the last eighteen years of her life living in Knoxville; it was longer than she had ever spent anywhere else. That November, during the weekend of a dangerous football riot across the river at UT, where the Vols beat Tulane, Ida Cox died. A tiny, standard obituary appeared in the local papers that Sunday, mentioning nothing about her recording career. The same day, the *New York Times* ran a much larger article about the death of Ida Cox. A week later, she made *Time* magazine's "Milestones" column.

Her family buried her at Longview Cemetery, an old, predominantly black graveyard on Keith Avenue that eventually went out of business. Her grave was apparently moved to New Gray, where it is now, near the grave of her daughter, Helen Goode, who died in 1992.

Cox wrote and sang several songs about graveyards, and as it happens, these two gravestones add another facet to the mystery of Ida Cox. If the inscribed birth dates are correct, Helen was born when her mother was only fourteen. According to Goode's newspaper obituary, Ida Cox's daughter was born in Cedartown, Georgia, the hometown Cox said she had fled forever when she was sixteen.

When Cox told Westergaard about running away from home, she didn't say anything about running away with a small child in tow. Her gravestone, flush with the mown grass, is unremarkable, except for the addition of one word: Mother.

The one-story frame house that she and her daughter shared on Louise Avenue stood for forty years after Cox's death but was torn down without notice in 2008.

# THE POET AND THE TERRORIST

During two years of violence beginning in the late summer of 1956, citizens rioted on the town square and attacked one another because of the color of their neighbors' skin. Dynamite bombs injured several in black neighborhoods in Anderson County, interrupted a Louis Armstrong performance in Knoxville and ultimately destroyed the entire Clinton High School. Clinton was, briefly, internationally famous.

Thanks to a federal court order handed down in Knoxville, in response to a six-year-old lawsuit, in 1956 Clinton High had become one of the first white public schools in the Jim Crow South to enroll black students. What followed is remembered, but only occasionally, as being among the most dramatic and violent events of the civil rights era in Tennessee and the setting of some of the earliest segregationist resistance in the South.

Similar stories would be replayed all over the South over the following decades, but none surpassed ours for the strangeness of the principal agitators. The two founders of the local White Citizens Council, who stirred up the crowds in Clinton and attempted to do the same in Knoxville, were from out of state. They weren't necessarily rednecks or provincial reactionaries. Both were college-educated young men who had lived in other parts of the country, and they could both have been described as literary intellectuals.

One would later make a fortune as a novelist and author of an endearing memoir of a Native American youth that became a national bestseller before scholars discovered the author's real identity.

The other, who had deeper influence here, was a former Greenwich Village bohemian, a protégé and close associate of the poet Ezra Pound. The elderly poet himself, accused of treason and confined in his cell in a mental institution, may have had more to do with the formation of the White Citizens Council, the rhetoric the agitators used to whip up the crowds—and the Clinton violence—than most historians of the civil rights era know.

The historic changes at Clinton High were six years in the making. In 1950, families of six black students had sued to get their kids into the all-white high school. At the time, the "separate but equal" statute was still credible to judges, and there wasn't case history to support the suit.

Then, a similar case out of Topeka, Kansas, made it to the U.S. Supreme Court in 1954, and the *Brown v. Board* decision ended legal segregation in America.

The first consequence of the Brown decision in Tennessee was Judge Robert Taylor's ruling in January 1956 that Clinton High would have to desegregate. It wasn't the only all-white school in the area, of course. All public schools were segregated. Even the University of Tennessee allowed no black undergraduates. Clinton High was different in a couple of regards, beginning with that early lawsuit and conditions that made the status quo especially absurd. Since there were no black high schools in Clinton, black Clinton kids had to be bussed all

Troops were called in to keep the peace in Clinton after rioting, much of it sparked by a former New York bookseller named John Kasper, who somehow became East Tennessee's most outspoken segregationist. *Courtesy of the Library of Congress.*

the way to Austin High in Knoxville, thirty miles away. It took a fair-minded judge to put it all together.

Bald by his mid-fifties and diminutive in height, Judge Robert Love Taylor was still known as "Little Bob." A few in 1956 were old enough to remember his uncle and namesake, "Our Bob" Taylor, the charismatic governor and senator of the Victorian era. The judge's own father, Alf Taylor, had once been governor, as well. Judge Taylor was acquainted with power and influence in his home state. He had enjoyed a brief career as a professional baseball player just after World War I. He had quit to go to Yale law school. Though his father had been Republican, Taylor had once promised his uncle, who let the boy sit in his chair in the U.S. Senate, that he would be a Democrat no matter what. Senator Taylor gave Little Bob a ten-dollar bill to seal the bargain. That was the story he told, anyway, and the affiliation paid off; in 1949, President Truman appointed Taylor a U.S. federal court judge in Tennessee's Eastern District.

The Democratic Party in Tennessee had no association with civil rights in 1956, but as a judge, Taylor was known as especially efficient and conscientious. He had a black bailiff, which was perhaps unusual in the 1950s South. Taylor was not remembered as unusually progressive for his time and was certainly not known as a judicial activist. When he ruled that Clinton High would have to desegregate, he was almost apologetic about it. He had no choice—the law's the law.

At first, it seemed as if the result of his ruling would be accepted by a calm populace in a historically calm town. It had been a quiet summer, and on Saturday, August 26, Clinton High enrolled twelve black students. They joined the seven hundred white students already there.

No one bothered them that day.

But just before that, on Friday, August 25, a strange young man drove into town. Though he was clean-cut and wore a suit and tie, he slept in his car that night. For the next fifty years, the people of Knoxville and Anderson County would claim that everything that happened in the weeks and months to come wouldn't have happened if John Kasper had not shown up.

Several Knoxvillians remembered Kasper even half a century later. Former U.S. court clerk Don Ferguson was a part-time reporter for United Press International at the time; he met Kasper, attended some of his rallies and covered his trial.

"He was a tall, ordinary-looking fellow—but a little warped, offbeat," Ferguson said. "What I remember about him is that he was so dedicated, so sincere about a project that struck me as being hopeless." Though many local whites in the area had grown up with segregation and were comfortable with it,

A standoff between blacks and whites over who should be allowed to attend school at Clinton High, which was, in 1956, one of the South's first high schools to desegregate. *Courtesy of the Library of Congress.*

by 1956 most had accepted that change was inevitable. This newcomer from up North was convinced otherwise.

With a long nose and deep-set eyes, Kasper was arguably handsome in a rodent-like sort of way. He stood out in many aspects among the farmers of Anderson County. He was a Columbia graduate, a former Greenwich Village bookstore owner once known to love jazz. He was well spoken, and in his suit he always looked reasonably sharp, even in the midst of a mob, even when handcuffed to a drunk.

Raised in New Jersey, Kasper had been the sometimes-rebellious son of a moderately successful engineer. He reportedly suffered some personality disorder for which his parents had him seek counseling. His education was desultory and included some time at Yankton College in South Dakota. He was never an impressive student but did well enough to graduate from Columbia with a BS in "general studies." Among his teachers was well-known poet and essayist Babette Deutsch, who may have introduced him to the work of a writer who would change his life. She later said that, at the time, she was troubled by the fact that the undergraduate seemed less interested in a famous American poet's poetry than in his right-wing political philosophies.

# This Obscure Prismatic City

After graduation, still in his early twenties, Kasper opened a bookstore in the Village. It was a peculiar one, named Make It New after a 1935 book of essays by Kasper's greatest living hero, the modernist poet he had studied at Columbia. By the time he arrived in Clinton, Kasper had spent six years visiting, corresponding with, studying the work of and—the word is not too strong—worshipping Ezra Pound.

The poet may be more famous today than he was in 1956, but even then he was already, to his many friends and admirers—who included writers Ernest Hemingway, T.S. Eliot and Robert Frost—a living legend. In recent years, he had had suffered some significant emotional and legal problems, but a few colleagues, including the poet William Carlos Williams, expected Pound to be the next recipient of the Nobel Prize for Literature.

Pound had turned his back on his Idaho home early in the century to spend most of his life in self-exile in Europe. The classic bohemian, carelessly clothed, his hair piled high, he was too contrary even for Gertrude Stein, who had never forgiven him for carelessly breaking one of the antique chairs in her famous salon in Paris. His face had a mournful, defiant cast to it, even when he was young and wore a cavalier's beard and mustache.

By the time of World War I, Pound was already well known among litterateurs for his experimental poetry, colored with inimitable lines like "Your mind and you are our Sargasso Sea" and "The apparition of these faces in the crowd / Petals on a wet, black bough." After the war, he was an integral part of what would be known as the Lost Generation, the postwar café society of bohemians living in Paris in the orbit of avant-garde writer Gertrude Stein. Pound was a close friend and supporter of Hemingway, F. Scott Fitzgerald, Marcel Duchamp, James Joyce and others. He practiced a new kind of poetry, free in form but often complicated and demanding of the reader.

Though he was well known and influential among literary sorts by the 1920s, it wasn't until the 1960s that Pound was widely anthologized, taught in university and even high school survey classes. He is a significant character in the posthumous 1964 Hemingway memoir *A Moveable Feast* and is mentioned in the Bob Dylan song "Desolation Row" as a remote academic, along with T.S. Eliot, "fighting in the captain's tower/ While calypso singers laugh at them." He has inspired a groaning shelf full of full-length biographies with titles like *A Serious Character, This Difficult Individual, The Roots of Treason* and *The Solitary Volcano.*

People who read those books will learn that his life had a dark side.

In 1925, at the age of forty, Pound began his life's work, the famously obscure *Cantos*. To read them in their entirety, one has to be able to read Italian, French, Latin, Greek and Chinese.

Always willful and eccentric, somehow the man who celebrated new realms of freedom in verse became preoccupied with Mussolini and the rising cause of Italian fascism. His right-wing tendencies perplexed his friends, then and for the next several decades. Pound became an Italian fascist and a propagandist for the Axis powers during World War II, jeering at American troops in radio broadcasts. In 1945, American forces arrested him for treason, which carried a potential death sentence.

Rightly or wrongly, by 1946 Pound had been determined to be insane and unfit for trial. Incarcerated at St. Elizabeth's, the famous mental institution in Washington, D.C., he finished his endless *Cantos*. He enjoyed entertaining old friends and young admirers with his stories and philosophies about everything from Confucianism to usury. Some called his cell "Ezuversity."

In the summer of 1950, the twenty-year-old student John Kasper began visiting Pound at St. Elizabeth's. They must have made an odd pair—the dapper young man and the disheveled poet, some forty-four years Kasper's senior, who rarely buttoned his shirt. According to Kasper, Pound was so taken with the young man's ideological kinship that at the end of their first meeting, he shouted, "Bravo for Kasp!" Over the next few years, Pound would refer fondly to Kasper as Kasp or sometimes "der Kasperl." Kasper called Pound "der Boss." He sometimes signed his letters with a swastika and repeatedly asked Pound what he should do with his life.

It was the beginning of a regular correspondence. Through most of the '50s, Pound and Kasper exchanged letters at least once a week. Pound biographer E. Fuller Torrey read the unpublished letters and found them "extraordinary, indicating a complete master-student relationship and an apparent willingness to do whatever Pound asked. Kasper worshiped Pound and believed that he possessed a wisdom which was divine in origin." Kasper, who began the correspondence formally, began imitating Pound's intuitive, freeform style.

Pound's side of the correspondence is mostly unknown. Some scholars, like English author Clive Webb, have attempted to find the letters to determine the extent of Pound's influence over Kasper and his actions in Clinton and elsewhere. (Professor Webb, of the University of Sussex, has been at work for years on a book about Kasper and the Clinton crisis.) In collaboration with another young Pound admirer, T.D. Horton, Kasper published the Square Dollar book series, Pound's handpicked literary canon, which the poet described as "a set of texts intended to foster the spirit of reverence for the intelligence working in nature." Among the eccentric publications were Pound's translation of Confucius and some of the work of some other thinkers he considered overlooked, including economic historian Alexander del Mar and naturalist Louis Agassiz.

And so Kasper opened his bookstore, Make It New, on Bleecker Street in New York's Greenwich Village. It was a very strange place.

In the mid-1950s, some who visited his store regarded the proprietor as a "liberal," and in some ways he could pass for one. Kasper befriended some artistic blacks in New York, including choreographer Ned Williams. He helped artist Ted Joans and his white wife find an apartment, not always an easy thing for a mixed-race couple in the '50s, even in New York. For a time, Kasper dated a black woman. A contemporary reporter wrote that Make It New was "a recognized center for the distribution of pro-Negro books and magazines and was patronized chiefly by Negroes and Negrophile whites." Kasper retained some odd reactionary prejudices nonetheless. He espoused the NAACP but didn't join because, he explained, it was run by Jews. Some describe his contempt for Jews as a sudden, almost pathological oddity in his personality that had not been apparent when he first opened the bookstore.

Kasper could have borrowed the tenets of his anti-Semitism from Pound; he believed that Jews controlled much of the world, and intended to control all of it, partly through lending and interest or, as Pound railed even in his poetry, usury. Though Kasper had professed an admiration for Adolf Hitler, he was not at the time a garden-variety white supremacist. He had also admired Stalin. A superficial student of Nietzsche, Kasper seems to have been preoccupied with the idea of power and that the weak should yield to the strong.

Even after he began expressing anti-Semitic ideas, Kasper insisted at his Sunday-night gatherings that blacks should assert themselves in American culture without imitating it. His black friends would remember how he expressed disgust for how blacks were being treated in the South in those early days of the civil rights movement.

All of that information comes from a contemporary interview by scholar James Rorty with several of Kasper's black friends. Other scholars have described Make It New more simply as a "right-wing bookstore" that offered "venomous Nazi literature." It apparently had that, too. By one account, Pound had to talk Kasper out of one retail stunt he had proposed: piling books on psychology on the floor and labeling it "Jewish Muck." A rare photo of the shop in that era shows a poster headed, "Pot smokers who want to quit. Correct use of the breathing exercises described in these books will give you ALL the remarkable sensations you can get from marijuana." It added, "It's not smart to use HEROIN. The reds have been using drugs as a POLITICAL weapon since 1927. Don't be a Rooseveltian dupe!" To Beat-era Greenwich Village, Kasper probably seemed more like a freak than a dangerous racist.

His cozy biracial Sunday-evening bull sessions broke up. Some imply that it was over Kasper's growing hostility toward Jews and Communists. He closed the store about the time he mounted a quixotic presidential campaign for Ezra Pound in 1956, the year President Eisenhower ran for reelection against Democrats Adlai Stevenson and UT graduate Senator Estes Kefauver. "Pound for Prez" stickers went up all over New York subways.

In late 1955, Kasper had moved to Washington, D.C., perhaps to be closer to Pound, and opened another bookstore on Wisconsin Avenue called Cadmus. He reportedly roomed with fellow Pound devotee and anti-Semitic conspiracy theorist Eustace Mullins, who wrote one of the first biographies of Pound. He is also one of the few Pound biographers who claim that Pound had nothing to do with what followed down South.

While living in Washington, probably thanks to his close association with America's most famous mental patient, Kasper somehow found his way in to testify before a Senate subcommittee considering a mental health bill. There, he made a plea for the poet's release. "We do not have the benefit of Ezra Pound," he said. "We cannot openly talk about him or claim him as an American poet because he is supposed to be insane." From there, he launched into his theory that psychology was a Jewish plot. When Senator Alan Bible asked him, "Are you opposed to the Jewish people?" Kasper responded, "I am opposed to any nation who attempts to usurp American nationality, and the Jews are nationalists of another country."

The bookstore apparently didn't work out, and by early 1956, Kasper, living near his idol and more focused than ever, finally had a cause.

Kasper founded something called the Seaboard White Citizens Council (SWCC), which may at one time have had a membership in the hundreds. Among its goals was the abolition of that subversive new music called rock 'n' roll. In fliers, Kasper designated himself as the SWCC's segregation chief. He hand-lettered pamphlets for distribution:

> *JAIL NAACP, alien, unclean, unchristian*
> *BLAST irreverent ungodly LEADERS*
> *HANG 9 SUPREME COURT SWINE*
> *(this year domine '56)*
> *Destroy REDS (ALL muscovite savages)*
> *rooseveltian dupes*
> *EXPOSE BERIA'S "psycho politics"*
> *DEATH TO USERERS.*

Many likely dismissed the screed as evidence of common schizophrenia. Later scholars would see the unmistakable influence of Ezra Pound. Some of the segregationist copy closely evoked a manifesto called *BLAST* written by Pound in collaboration with Wyndham Lewis in London in the Dadaist days of 1914.

"The phrases in his publicity had a distinctly Poundian ring," wrote literary scholar John Tytel in 1987, "and it was clear that Kasper had been counseled by his mentor."

Prior to 1956, Kasper's main association with the South was that he'd spent one year in the early '40s at a Georgia military academy, apparently a parent-suggested response to some personality problem, a solution that didn't work out. About 1955, he had tried to get work at Black Mountain College, near Asheville, but was unsuccessful. At some point, he befriended John G. Crommelin, the Alabama rear admiral suspended from duty for leaking classified information. In the postwar years, he became known as a segregationist and McCarthyist. Kasper told people that he had been campaign director for one of Crommelin's unsuccessful runs for U.S. Senate.

Whether it was Pound, Crommelin or some other agent, something persuaded Kasper, in the spring of 1956, to cross into the still-segregated South. He spent some time in Alabama, where he became acquainted with a radio personality named Asa, or "Ace," Carter, leader of a wing of the Alabama White Citizens Council so radical that Carter split away from that state's mainstream segregationists.

Kasper later went to Charlottesville, Virginia, where he released a pamphlet called *Virginians Awake!*, apparently to tepid response.

From there he drove straight to Clinton. One of the South's first attempts to desegregate a public high school presented an early battleground in what would be a national struggle.

He wasted no time. The day Kasper arrived, he went right to work, canvassing the countryside of Anderson County, knocking on doors. One of his pamphlets showed black GIs kissing French prostitutes at the end of World War II. He had allegedly obtained the photograph from Pound. This, Kasper explained, is what will happen if Clinton High desegregates.

"We are an action program," Kasper's pamphlet said. "We proclaim action as our creed. We are fighting. You must fight with us."

He baffled some of his subjects, by one account "talking a marvelously impressive hodgepodge of Blackstone, Douglas, Frobenius, Ezra Pound, and Joe Kamp." Most reportedly thought him a Yankee kook, and some called the authorities. Within a few days, Kasper was jailed briefly for vagrancy.

But he stirred up enough to organize a picket line at the school and, within days, to bring people out to the town square in the hundreds.

Kasper's strength, according to scholar and journalist Rorty, was among "the poor people of Anderson County, who have been left with so little else with which to nourish their pride that their membership in the master race has become their most precious possession." Kasper spoke to crowds without notes, spewing invective at Jews and blacks and claiming desegregation to be a Communist plot. Some noticed that he apparently wasn't used to using the word "nigger" and frequently corrected himself to include it.

Though some contemporary journalists like Rorty had the impression that Kasper stirred up the trouble "almost single-handedly," he couldn't have done so without willing allies in Anderson County. He got about fifty students to lay out of school and join the picket line. A group called the Tennessee White Youth made up uniform shirts emblazoned with Confederate flags. One Clinton mother explained why she was keeping her kids out of school: "Before I'd raise [my children] up with a nigger, I'd raise 'em up dumb as I am."

The mob chased away black students and their families. The tiny police department was helpless. A group of concerned citizens pleaded with Judge Taylor to issue an order barring Kasper and five local collaborators from further action, and Mayor W.E. Lewallen asked state authorities to enforce the laws with the National Guard.

By Friday night, Kasper's Alabama friend Ace Carter arrived to address a throng of fifteen hundred in front of the courthouse that had been bashing cars containing black passengers. In contrast to Kasper's scholarly look, Carter was a broad, moonfaced fellow with heavy, dark eyebrows and a five o'clock shadow it took more than a shave to hide. He was the kind of man a crowd like this could respect; he looked mean as a wrestler.

Kasper later called Carter "the only sincere and courageous leader in the entire movement." The sincerity issue would come up later in Carter's career.

At one point, the star-struck crowd chanted "We Want Kasper!" Clinton's seven policemen prevented them from attacking the home of the mayor. Mainly, they watched.

The mayor deputized an emergency posse of citizens, armed with everything from old Nazi weapons to shotguns and a few machine guns to tear gas grenades on loan from Mayor Jack Dance in Knoxville.

When the posse arrived, a crowd of three thousand welcomed it with shouts of "Let's kill the nigger-lovers! Kill them!" The posse advanced and lobbed a tear gas grenade—fortunately, just as the first cars of the highway patrol arrived to help enforce order. By the time it was over, there were tanks on the town square, one hundred highway patrolmen and six hundred national guardsmen.

Joe Wilson, Clinton's acting police chief, said, "I firmly believe that none of this would have happened if outsiders had stayed away. We here in Clinton can settle our problems without help from any outside agitators." As early as August 31, a *Knoxville Journal* story reported, "Officers and school officials alike blame most of the trouble on a 26-year-old Washington man named John Kasper." At one point, Kasper, freed from jail, had the opportunity to shout to Principal D.J. Brittain, before several onlookers, "I will get the niggers out of the schools, or you out."

In Knoxville, Judge Taylor slapped Kasper with a one-year contempt-of-court sentence, an unusually tough sentence for a judge to impose at his discretion without a jury trial. A news photo showed the arrested Kasper grinning in handcuffs. He quickly raised the $10,000 bail. He was unapologetic. He resented the use of troops to quell his mob. "Woe to those whose only right is their power," he said. "The wild grass will grow over their dead bodies."

Touring the South, the former bookseller told a large crowd in Birmingham that September:

> *I'm a rabble-rouser, a troublemaker. I'm not through up there. We want trouble. We want it now. Some of us may die and I may die, too. It may mean going back to jail, but I'm going back to fight. We went as far as we could have gone legally. Now is the time to fight, even if it involves bloodshed.*

He enjoyed his moment. "I have been interested all my life in the purity of races," he told a local reporter. "I do not hate Negroes, but I believe that for the progress of the white and Negro races this is best accomplished by segregated institutions." On September 24, Kasper and Carter tried to bring the fight into Knox County.

The prospect alarmed many Knoxvillians. Mayor Dance said that he wouldn't permit them to convene within the city. They made plans to meet at Fountain City Park, which was then outside city limits. By some accounts, it was a Fountain City attorney, John Webb Green, instrumental in founding the park, who stopped them. Son of a Confederate officer killed in the Civil War, Green was then in his nineties and was known to be annoyed by those who unrealistically glorified the Old South. He found a way to legally block Kasper and Carter's appearance at his beloved Fountain City Park as a disturbance of the peace.

Sheriff Paul Lilly warned Carter that he would be arrested if he set foot in Fountain City Park. Kasper and Carter met on the shoulder of North Broadway, across a ditch from the park. A crowd of only two to three hundred people showed up on the rainy afternoon, a disappointment after the throngs in Clinton. Carter blamed the bad weather and "an excellent

Segregationist John Kasper, escorted in handcuffs, at the time of his federal trial outside the post office building in downtown Knoxville. At the time, Ernest Hemingway was urging his old friend Ezra Pound to deny any involvement with Kasper. Pound refused. *Calvin McClung Historical Collection.*

hatchet job by the press. They fixed us good." Carter tried to give it a spin to make it a little victory in the propaganda war, even if he had to mix some metaphors to get there. The SWCC had "forced those in power to show their teeth, and it doesn't look very nice when the velvet glove is off and the iron fist exposed."

On November 5, while awaiting trial for sedition and inciting to riot, Kasper gave a speech on temperance. Observers noted that he wasn't as impassioned on that subject and spoke from notes. He made room to criticize "jive music" on the radio and Tennessee governor Frank Clement.

# This Obscure Prismatic City

On November 20, a Clinton jury found Kasper not guilty of sedition and incitement to riot. But it wasn't over for Kasper. He and fifteen others faced trial on federal charges of conspiracy. They would be called "the Clinton 16." One of them, a Clinton restaurant owner, survived a couple of suicide attempts but died at Eastern State Psychiatric Hospital of undisclosed causes.

The Clinton riots got worldwide coverage. In the Soviet Union, Pravda showed photographs of this "new, wild orgy of racists" in America, as did Communist papers in East Berlin, under the heading "The Mob Reigns in Tennessee." It was their favorite kind of story.

In early December, a white mob attacked the Reverend Paul Turner, a white preacher who had been escorting black children to school. He was beaten severely.

The *New York Herald Tribune* published the story under the surprising headline: "Segregationist Kasper is Ezra Pound Disciple." A few weeks later, *Look* magazine published a large feature about the Clinton riots with photographs of both Kasper and Pound and a brief interview with Kasper's mother in New Jersey. "When you have a child," she said, "you don't know how it's going to turn out." Meanwhile, Pound's old friends, struggling to get him released from the incarceration that had started as a capital treason charge, were dumbfounded. Poet William Carlos Williams claimed that he had never heard of Kasper before the news reports of the Clinton association, which seemed to be undermining what remained of Pound's tenuous reputation.

Kasper, awaiting trial for conspiracy, continued to work vigorously, and it was only natural that he would get back into publishing. Here, in February 1957, Kasper began publishing the *Clinton-Knox County Stars and Bars*: "A Nationalist Attack Newspaper Serving East Tennessee." Pound scholars see echoes of the poet's work in the local paper, which called for "local control of local purchasing-power" and condemned "interest slavery." Sometimes Kasper cribbed Pound straight, as in the line: "The right aim of law is to prevent coercion, either by force or fraud." His ostensibly local paper also pleaded for "the immediate release from an 11-year political imprisonment of Ezra Pound: America's greatest poet, man of letters, and leader in the life-death struggle against deadly usury." He condemned Clare Booth Luce, U.S. ambassador to Italy, for not doing enough to ensure Pound's release.

Weirder things kept happening. Kasper began using new imagery in his spiels. "I say that integration can be reversed," he said in early 1957. "It has got to be a pressure down here which is more or less like a lit stick of dynamite and you throw it in their laps and let them catch it, and then they can do what they want with it, but let them worry about it." It sounded like a metaphor.

119

That month, jazz legend Louis Armstrong and his mixed-race band performed before an audience of both blacks and whites in segregated seating at Chilhowee Park. Someone driving slow past the park lobbed a dynamite bomb from a car. It interrupted the show briefly, but no one was hurt. "Don't worry, folks, it's just the telephone," an unflappable Armstrong said of the noise outside. The bombing, which left a hole in the lawn, was ascribed to the White Citizens Council. Kasper was suspected of involvement but never charged.

It was one of the first of several dynamite bombings, most of them in and around Clinton; some of them were suitcase bombs left in the middle of the night. One in a black neighborhood injured three, but none seriously.

Meanwhile, there was an unexpected personal development in the Kasper case. It had been reported that Kasper had run a "right-wing bookstore" in New York, and his segregationist pals down South were apparently OK with that. But Kasper's nationwide notoriety had turned up some surprising old, but not very old, interior photographs of Make It New. One photo, published in the *Knoxville Journal* and other papers, shows a group of blacks and whites that appears to include a couple of biracial couples, their arms around each other. Kasper is right in the midst of them, beaming happily. By then, word that he had befriended and even dated blacks was getting around. There was another report that Kasper had participated in African tribal dancing. Suddenly, he was no longer a hero in Alabama.

"I realize I present a real problem to the segregationist cause," Kasper admitted to the press. "People don't understand. It's just one place where people have to make a mental leap to see the picture. If they can't make the leap, they'll just work their way and I can work mine." His credibility as the new hero of the right-wing South may have ended on the day those photographs were published.

The federal conspiracy trial, held in the federal courthouse and post office on Main Street in Knoxville, drew attention from all over. The defense had a team of hotshot lawyers from across the South, some of them known segregationists. On the team was Ross Barnett, the future hardcore segregationist governor of Mississippi, known for his belief that the black race was cursed by God.

The jury was composed entirely of whites. When the one prospective black juror admitted that he "couldn't feel kindly" about Kasper, he was dismissed. The trial lasted several days and featured more than 120 witnesses, including Admiral Crommelin, who came to say nice things about Kasper. The defense skillfully prevented introduction of some evidence and was confident of acquittal.

The decision came back quickly—two hours of discussion and one ballot. It was, everyone agreed, a surprise.

A surprising photo of John Kasper (in rear) in his earlier life as a Greenwich Village bookseller. This image, taken inside his bookstore, Make It New, around 1955, surfaced during the controversy about his part in leading white supremacist rallies in Tennessee during the late 1950s, perplexing many on both sides of the struggle. *Calvin McClung Historical Collection.*

Several were acquitted, but Kasper and six codefendants, most of them working-class Anderson County people who were much older than Kasper, were found guilty.

Don Ferguson later remembered how Kasper replied to Judge Taylor's routine question, the last chance for the convicted defendant to say something in his defense before receiving his sentence. Usually, defendants try to sound contrite.

"Yes," Kasper responded. "I plead with you to order the Negroes out of Clinton High School."

Taylor gave him another year. He remained free for a time, pending appeals, and moved to Nashville, where he got in more trouble. He was eventually accused of conspiring to bomb an elementary school.

\*\*\*

Ezra Pound had become known as the "national skeleton." By the mid-1950s, even Tokyo Rose, the Axis propagandist whose radio broadcasts reached much farther than Pound's ever did, had been freed. But Pound was an old poet in his seventies, held as if he were a danger to society. Some argued that Kasper was doing all he could to prove that he still was a danger to society.

Pound's exasperated friends, attempting to get the elderly poet free of St. Elizabeth's, were frustrated with his association with Kasper and Tennessee.

In July 1957, writers Archibald MacLeish and Robert Frost made a plea to the Justice Department and Eisenhower administration attorney general William Rogers. Considering the Pound dilemma, Rogers said that his greatest anxiety about freeing the elderly poet was that "Pound might join Kasper in the South and people would be killed."

When MacLeish asked Pound whether he was actually helping Kasper, the old man didn't reply directly. "I doubt if Kasper hates anyone," Pound said elliptically. "His actions in keeping open shack for stray cats and humans seem to indicate a kind heart, with no exclusion of Nubians."

Frustrated with the prospects for an imminent release, MacLeish wrote to Pound, frankly:

> For the immediate future and so long as the Kasper mess is boiling and stewing the Department will not move. I have never understood—and, incidentally, neither has your daughter, Mar—how you got mixed up with that character. We were left with the impression that once the Kasper stink has blown over they would be willing to consider proposals.

If Pound himself ever regretted his association with Kasper, it is not clear in the biographies. "Well, at least he's a man of action, and don't sit around looking at his navel," said Pound.

Ernest Hemingway was especially concerned. He donated $1,500, which he said was the last of his Nobel Prize money, to the effort to free his old friend from St. Elizabeth's. Hemingway wrote to MacLeish that Pound's "megalomania makes him receive dangerous fawning jerks such as Kasper." He privately admitted that he was afraid that Pound, if released, would go to the press and praise Kasper's segregationist efforts in Tennessee—that Pound would "go on the Mike Wallace show" and get himself in trouble all over again.

In the literary journal *Paris Review* in the spring of 1958, Hemingway wrote, "I believe Ezra should be released and allowed to write poetry in Italy on an understanding by him to abstain from any politics. I would be happy to see Kasper jailed as soon as possible." Some thought that John Kasper in jail would mean freedom for Ezra Pound.

Hemingway got his wish: Kasper, out of appeals, was finally imprisoned in May 1958 at the federal penitentiary in Atlanta. He was seen carrying a copy of *Mein Kampf* into the penitentiary.

Days earlier, Pound had been released from St. Elizabeth's. He immediately returned to Italy. Biographers believe that his association with Kasper and the Clinton mess delayed the poet's release from the mental institution by about a year.

Pound offered no evidence of contrition. As his ship arrived in Naples, he posed for reporters, grinning and offering the stiff-armed fascist salute.

Kasper at least occasionally stayed in touch with Pound. In October 1958, he wrote to Pound in Italy, boasting that seven synagogues in the South had been bombed. In April 1959, Pound reportedly wrote back, "Stick to the main points when possible. Antisemitism is a card in the enemy program. Don't play it. They RELY on your playing it."

In the same month that Kasper crowed to Pound about bombed synagogues, dynamite bombs ripped Clinton High School apart. The perpetrators weren't obvious, and since Kasper hadn't been in town recently, he wasn't implicated. His lawyers may have been relieved that their client was in the penitentiary at the time and, for once, had an alibi.

The gymnasium remained, barely. Billy Graham spoke there to a shaken community that December.

After a spell in federal penitentiaries in Atlanta and Florida, Kasper served six months in a Nashville workhouse for a conviction on conspiracy to blow up an elementary school there.

Kasper returned to Knoxville for a weird final campaign in April 1959, against city-county consolidation, of all things. "Metro is communist inspired," he said. "Metro is evil. Hate Metro. Vote no to Metro." This time, Knox County went Kasper's way.

Kasper dropped out of the local news but was not quite forgotten, like an especially peculiar nightmare. In 1960, Martin Luther King visited Knoxville College, and within weeks, nonviolent activists were participating in sit-ins. Knoxville restaurants began to desegregate without major incident. Some liked it, some didn't, but there were no riots and no bombings.

In March 1961, *Knoxville Journal* writer Ray Flowers walked into a bar and happened to spot an "intent" John Kasper, free and drinking a beer. He was wearing a dark suit and said that he was just visiting friends. He said he had been treated well in prison and that he'd given up violence.

"The answer to the integration problem lies in a return of constitutionalism," he told Flowers. "Continuance of my previous methods which landed me in jail would be useless Don Quixoteism."

He said that he was working on three books, one an autobiography of his segregationist activities and trials; one on the Jacksonian period, which Flowers said Kasper "considers the golden age of the United States"; and one about "Ezra Pound, the fascist poet."

"He indicated that writing books might be a better way to fight for his opinions than rabble-rousing...He seemed genuinely pleased to be recognized, but demonstrated extreme nervousness," Flowers wrote. "His eyes constantly darted about the tavern, and he was easily startled. He talked of nothing but his favorite subject for an hour or so...At midnight he was heard to inquire where he might go to get another beer."

With that gesture, John Kasper walked out of his strange chapter in Knoxville history.

He spent much of the rest of his life in Nashville, apparently keeping his word about working through the system. He ran unsuccessfully for state representative in 1962.

Then, as if to make Pound's 1956 "campaign" seem credible by comparison, Kasper ran for president, on the so-called National States' Rights Party (NSRP) ticket, with segregationist terrorist J.B. Stoner, a Chattanooga native who was later convicted for a Birmingham church bombing, as his running mate. (Some sources note that the extreme right-wing party, whose neo-Nazi message was too radical for most southern segregationists, was founded in Knoxville in 1958, doubtless with Kasper's help.) It was 1964, the year of the Johnson-Goldwater race. Though the NSRP's motto was "America's Largest Third Party," a somehow un-emboldened Kasper, who reportedly didn't even campaign, earned only three thousand votes nationwide. Today, Kasper-Stoner buttons sell on e-Bay for about five bucks.

Kasper reportedly stayed in touch with the self-exiled Pound by mail, at least until 1962. The poet never won the Nobel Prize. Though free in his beloved Italy, Pound's final years were not happy ones, as he struggled with disease, depression and the dilemma of whether to live with his long-suffering wife or his long-suffering mistress. But judging by the abundance of photographs of him as an old man, he enjoyed posing for a picture. He died in 1971, at the age of eighty-six.

Pound's connections to Kasper were only occasionally mentioned in the Knoxville press and never with much emphasis or elaboration. Perhaps local reporters found the association too esoteric. Pound's name was not as widely recognized as it would be a little later when his work was widely anthologized in freshman survey classes and Pound himself was highlighted in famous memoirs, Dylan songs and numerous full-length biographies.

Still, to this day, many otherwise comprehensive civil rights histories that describe Kasper don't mention Pound—though almost all biographies of Pound offer extensive discussions of Kasper. Scholars are uncertain of the extent of Pound's influence over Kasper and the events of 1956–58. "While there is no evidence that Pound told Kasper to go and do the things he did," wrote Australian critic Noel Stock near the end of Pound's life, "there is plenty of evidence that he used him for his own purposes during the early 1950s and was a contributing factor to his later excesses."

Some make Pound sound like the Svengali of the Clinton riots. Others make him seem like an innocent, albeit perverse, bystander. Pound's degree of influence may become clear if Pound's letters to Kasper are ever found and released.

Kasper's later years aren't as well documented as Pound's, but Kasper's activism seems to have evaporated soon after his correspondence with Pound ended.

After that eight-year burst of extreme fame, Kasper disappeared from sight. Whether he ever published any of the books he described to the *Journal* reporter is unclear. Like his colleague Ace Carter, with whom he had talked so tough in Clinton, Kasper changed his first name in the mid-1960s, about the time the Civil Rights Act and Voting Rights Act signified an end to the segregationist era. Kasper was known for the rest of his life by his first name: Fred. He apparently went through a couple of divorces.

Several people I spoke to in Knoxville had significantly different opinions of Kasper's fate: that he died young, or in Florida or Mississippi, or that Kasper was maybe still alive. Social Security records indicate that Frederick John Kasper died in April 1998, at the age of sixty-eight. Some children and ex-wives survive him.

Kasper's story has no parallel in American history. But a stranger coda in the story belongs to Ace Carter, the tough-talking Alabama segregationist who led segregationist demonstrations in Clinton and Fountain City alongside Kasper.

In 1976, an author named Forrest Carter, already famous for a book called *The Outlaw Josie Wales*, on which a popular Clint Eastwood western about a former Confederate turned desperado was based, wrote a different sort of book: a memoir about a Native American childhood. It was called *The Education of Little Tree*. Reprinted in 1986, it became a heartwarming bestseller, praised as a bridge between the white and Native American races. There was a tragic poignancy to the story that Carter had not lived to enjoy the fullness of his success. He died in 1979 at the age of fifty-three, allegedly after a fistfight with his son.

In 1991, scholars discovered that the author, Forrest Carter, was born by the name Asa Carter and had once been a white supremacist of an especially angry sort. He had been a member of the Ku Klux Klan and had written pro-segregation speeches for George Wallace, allegedly including the famous "Segregation Forever" speech. Before that, the surprising news reports went, he had been a radio hatemonger who had stirred up the crowds down in Tennessee.